P9-EFJ-400

DATE DUE

OCT 1 2 1988	
NOV 1 0 1988	
NOV 2 8 1988	
MAY 4 1989	
MAR 7 1990	
APR 2 1990	
APR 1 8 1991	
DEC 1 8 1992	
MAR 0 6 1998	
APR 1 0 1998	
APR 2 8 2005	

DORIS LESSING

LITERATURE AND LIFE SERIES
(Formerly Modern Literature and World Dramatists)

Selected list of titles:

JAMES BALDWIN	Carolyn Wedin Sylvander
ANTHONY BURGESS	Samuel Coale
TRUMAN CAPOTE	Helen S. Garson
WILLA CATHER	Dorothy Tuck McFarland
T.S. ELIOT	Burton Raffel
E.M. FORSTER	Claude J. Summers
ERNEST HEMINGWAY	Samuel Shaw
JOHN IRVING	Gabriel Miller
CHRISTOPHER ISHERWOOD	Claude J. Summers
HENRY JAMES, THE NOVELS OF	Edward Wagenknecht
HENRY JAMES, THE TALES OF	Edward Wagenknecht
KEN KESEY	Barry H. Leeds
ARTHUR KOESTLER	Mark Levene
D.H. LAWRENCE	George J. Becker
MARY MCCARTHY	Willene Schaefer Hardy
NORMAN MAILER	Philip H. Bufithis
JOHN O'HARA	Robert Emmet Long
EUGENE O'NEILL, THE PLAYS OF	Virginia Floyd
GEORGE ORWELL	Roberta Kalechofsky
EDGAR ALLAN POE	Bettina L. Knapp
MURIEL SPARK	Velma Bourgeois Richmond
JOHN STEINBECK	Paul McCarthy
LIONEL TRILLING	Edward Joseph Shoben, Jr.
MARK TWAIN	Robert Keith Miller
GORE VIDAL	Robert F. Kiernan
ROBERT PENN WARREN	Katherine Snipes
EDMUND WILSON	David Castronovo
THOMAS WOLFE	Elizabeth Evans
VIRGINIA WOOLF	Manly Johnson

Complete list of titles in the series available from publisher on request.

DORIS LESSING

Mona Knapp

FREDERICK UNGAR PUBLISHING CO.
New York

Copyright © 1984 by Frederick Ungar Publishing Co., Inc.
Printed in the United States of America

Library of Congress Cataloging in Publication Data

Knapp, Mona.
　　Doris Lessing.

　　Bibliography: p.
　　Includes index.
　　1. Lessing, Doris May, 1919-　　　—Criticism and
interpretation.　　I. Title.
PR6023.E833Z735　1984　　　823'.914　　　84-131
ISBN 0-8044-2491-8
ISBN 0-8044-6372-7 (pbk.)

Acknowledgments

Excerpt from the play *Each His Own Wilderness* reprinted by permission of Penguin Books Ltd. (from *New English Dramatists*, ed. E. Martin Browne. Harmondsworth, Middlesex: Penguin Books, 1959, p. 95). Copyright © 1959 by Doris Lessing.

Poetry excerpt from *Briefing For a Descent Into Hell* quoted by permission of Alfred A. Knopf, Inc., Copyright © 1971 by Doris Lessing.

Poetry excerpt from "New Man,"Copyright © 1959 Doris Lessing. Reprinted by permission of Jonathan Clowes Ltd., London, on behalf of Doris Lessing.

For Nina and Hanna

We are living at a time which is so dangerous, violent, explosive, and precarious that it is in question whether soon there will be people left alive to write books and to read them. It is a question of life and death for all of us; and we are haunted, all of us, by the threat that even if some madman does not destroy us all, our children may be born deformed or mad. We are living at one of the great turning points of history. In the last two decades man has made an advance as revolutionary as when he first got off his belly and stood upright. Yesterday, we split the atom. We assaulted that colossal citadel of power, the tiny unit of the substance of the universe. And because of this, the great dream and the great nightmare of centuries of human thought have taken flesh and walk beside us all, day and night. . . . What is the choice before us? It is not merely a question of preventing an evil, but of strengthening a vision of a good which may defeat the evil.

—Doris Lessing, "The Small Personal Voice," 1957

Who knows but that beings are not moved about among the planets, in one shape or another, as plants are moved about in a garden, or even taken indoors when frost is expected? . . . For we may suppose, I am sure, that Planets are altogether gentler and more humane than poor beast Man, lifting his bloody muzzle to his lurid sky, to howl out his misery and his exhaustion in between battles with his kind.

—Doris Lessing, *Briefing For a Descent Into Hell*, 1971

Contents

Preface

This study is intended as a general introduction to the entire works of Doris Lessing, one of the most important English-language writers living today. Though its main object is to provide reading guidelines for the student and nonspecialist, I also hope that Lessing scholars may find food for thought here and, in keeping with the spirit of Lessing's work, a few bones for critical contention.

In a career now spanning nearly thirty-five years, Doris Lessing has written many thousands of pages, and her productivity is still undiminished. The necessary evils involved in an introduction to a work of this scope are obvious: it must not only simplify, generalize and skim surfaces, but also map out linear developments which may appear artificial and arbitrary. Further, it can only offer ad interim conclusions regarding those books whose very essence attests to the necessity of constant flux and change. Roughly following the chronology of Lessing's novel production, this study begins with her first one (1950) and ends with her most recent publication (1983). Deviations from chronology were necessary to accommodate short stories (chapters 2 and 4), poems and plays (chapter 3), as well as the essays (chapter 8), which I have grouped for simplicity's sake by genre. For ease of reference to quotations, I have cited wherever possible the pagination of the paperback editions which are most likely to be purchased by the general reader. Exceptions are made for out-of-print works and those not available in paperback. Discussions of individual works aim primarily at the illumination of crucial interpretative issues. As far as possible without engaging in tiresome plot-retelling, the interpretations are structured to make each book's content clear to those readers who may be unfamiliar with it. Limitations of space made certain simplifications or ellipses in this regard unavoidable; for the finer points of plot progression the reader is referred to any of the detailed studies listed in the bibliography and, of course, to the texts themselves. Within the framework of this study, I could not aspire to take issue with or even to cite most of the secondary works on Lessing to date. This would be the task of a more specialized investigation—a task made challenging and fruitful by the highly diverse talents and specialties of Lessing's critics. Nor could I document all primary quotations; I have however provided page numbers for the majority according to length and importance. Understanding only too well the plight of quotation seekers, I apologize for any omissions.

I wish to thank many friends and colleagues, as well as those libraries and archives on two continents, who have assisted my research. My heartfelt thanks go to Doris Lessing for her gracious and generous assistance in clarifying biographical details. All errors, naturally, are my own. I am grateful to Philip Winsor for his expert and meticulous editorial hand, and to Frederick Ungar for his always energetic backing of literature and its critics. Most especially I thank my daughters for patience and moral support that go far beyond their years; and my husband, for whose untiring encouragement and painstaking criticism no thanks can be adequate.

Salt Lake City, April 1983

Chronology

1919   Doris May Tayler is born on October 22 in Kermanshah, Persia (today Iran), the first child of Emily Maude (nee McVeagh) Tayler and Alfred Cook (called Michael) Tayler, British citizens. Tayler is a bank official with the Imperial Bank of Persia.

1921   Doris's brother Harry, the Taylers' second child born.

1924   The Tayler family emigrates to Southern Rhodesia.

1926-32   Doris attends school at the Roman Catholic Convent in Salisbury.

1932-33   She spends one year at the Girls' High School in Salisbury, which concludes her formal schooling. Her education thereafter consists of extensive independent reading.

1934-36   Doris Tayler does household work as an *au pair* girl with two families in Salisbury.

1936-37   First efforts to write prose and poetry result in two novels and several novel fragments (unpublished).

1938   She takes final departure from her
            parents' farm to seek work in Salis-
            bury. Her first job is with the tele-
            phone company as an operator.

1939   Marriage at age nineteen to Frank
            Charles Wisdom, a civil servant.

1942   Doris Wisdom becomes involved in a
            local Marxist group.

1943   Divorce from Frank Wisdom, who
            retains custody of their son John and
            daughter Jean. First poems and short
            fiction are published in local journals.

1945   Marriage to Gottfried Anton Lessing, a
            German refugee and fellow-member
            of the Marxist group in which she is
            active. D. Lessing works as a typist for
            two legal offices, then for government
            commissions and Hansard, the official
            Parliament Record.

1947   Birth of Lessing's third child, Peter.

1947-48   Lessing works on *The Grass is Singing*
            and forms plans to emigrate to En-
            gland.

1949   Divorce from Gottfried Lessing, who
            returns to Germany. Doris Lessing sails
            with her son Peter to London.

1950   Her first novel, *The Grass is Singing*, is
            published.

1951   *This Was the Old Chief's Country*,
        short stories, is published.

1952   *Martha Quest*, Lessing's second novel
        and the initial volume of the *Children
        of Violence* series. Lessing is a partici-
        pant in a delegation of the Authors'
        World Peace Appeal to the Soviet
        Union.

1953   *Five: Short Novels*. Lessing's first play,
        Before the Deluge (also known under
        the title *Mr. Dolinger*) is produced in
        London.

1954   *A Proper Marriage*, Lessing's third novel
        (volume two of *Children of Violence*)
        is published. Lessing receives the
        Somerset Maugham Award of the
        Society of Authors for *Five*.

1956   Lessing returns to Africa after seven
        years' absence. She has in the mean-
        time been declared a "prohibited im-
        migrant" because of her political views,
        but is admitted by mistake. On her
        return to England, she formally leaves
        the Communist party in protest against
        Stalinist atrocities and the invasion of
        Hungary. *Retreat to Innocence*, her
        fourth novel, is published.

1957   *Going Home*, an autobiographical
        reportage describing her trip to Africa;
        The Habit of Loving (short stories).

1958   Her fifth novel, *A Ripple From the*

Storm (volume three of *Children of Violence*). A second play, *Each His Own Wilderness*, is performed by the English Stage Society at the Royal Court Theatre, London, on 23 March. *Mr. Dolinger* produced in Oxford.

1959   *Fourteen Poems* and *Each His Own Wilderness* published.

1960   Publication of *In Pursuit of the English*, Lessing's second major autobiographical essay. Third play, *The Truth About Billy Newton*, produced in Salisbury, Wiltshire.

1962   ✳Publication of *The Golden Notebook*, Lessing's sixth novel, brings her overnight fame. Fourth drama, *Play With a Tiger*, produced in London. *The Grass is Singing* is adapted as a television play.

1963   *A Man and Two Women* (short stories).

1964   *African Stories* published. *Play With a Tiger* produced in New York. Lessing begins her studies of the mystical Islamic religion known as Sufism through the teachings of Idries Shah.

1965   *Landlocked*, seventh novel and volume four of *Children of Violence*.

1966   Lessing's literal translation of *The Storm*, a play by Alexander Ostrovsky, is produced unsuccessfully by the

National Theatre in London. Production of two original television plays, *Please Do Not Disturb* and *Care and Protection*. Lessing collaborates on further television scripts based on works by Maupassant.

1967   *Particularly Cats* (autobiographical essay); *Between Men*, a fourth television play adapted from the short story of the same title.

1969   *The Four-Gated City*, Lessing's eighth novel, completes her first novel sequence *Children of Violence*. Tour to United States includes visits to college campuses, among them SUNY Buffalo and Stony Brook, and Berkeley.

1971   *Briefing For a Descent Into Hell*, ninth novel.

1972·   *The Story of a Non-Marrying Man and Other Stories*.

1973   *The Summer Before the Dark*, tenth novel. Publication of a sixth drama, *The Singing Door*, a one-act play written for a textbook anthology. *The Sun Between Their Feet* and *This Was the Old Chief's Country* (complete African stories).

1974   Second trip to the United States. *The Memoirs of a Survivor*, Lessing's eleventh novel. *A Small Personal Voice* (collected essays).

1976   Lessing is awarded the Prix Medici for
         Foreigners (France).

1978   Publication of *To Room Nineteen* and
         The Temptation of Jack Orkney (com-
         plete British stories).

1979   *Shikasta*, Lessing's twelfth novel, is the
         first volume of a new series, *Canopus
         in Argos: Archives*.

1980   *The Marriages Between Zones Three,
         Four, and Five*, volume two of *Cano-
         pus in Argos* and Lessing's thirteenth
         novel.

1981   *The Sirian Experiments*, the author's
         fourteenth novel and volume three of
         the new series.

1982   *The Making of the Representative for
         Planet 8*, volume four of *Canopus* and
         Lessing's fifteenth novel.
           Lessing receives the Shakespeare Prize
         of the West German Hamburger Stif-
         tung. She is also awarded the Austrian
         State Prize for European Literature,
         given yearly to a literary figure of
         international significance. Trip to Spain
         in April. Second trip to Africa from
         July to September. Two week tour of
         Japan in November.

1983   Publication of *The Sentimental Agents*,
         fifth volume of *Canopus* and Lessing's
         sixteenth novel. Third trip to U.S.
         planned for spring of 1984.

1984   Third U.S.A.-tour in April.

DORIS LESSING

1

This Business of Being an Exile: Doris Lessing's Life and Works

It would be difficult to name any contemporary writer championed by so heterogeneous a readership as Doris Lessing. Her works are held in high esteem by young and old, mystics and arch-realists, feminists and anti-feminists; by readers in socialist and capitalist countries alike. They are sought out by bookworms and by people who "don't like literature." Lessing, it seems, thwarts the "isms" that would otherwise divide her readership. This is the natural result of her books' focus, unchanged for over thirty years: they attack compartmentalized thinking and strive toward a vision of the whole rather than the particular. In doing so, her works can be said to embrace all the "tensions and the disorientations that have marked the intellectual life of the west in the second half of the century."[1] From the early realist works to the newest space fantasies, Lessing's writings consistently provoke thought and enlarge the reader's perceptions by questioning the validity of labels and pigeonholes.

The deep distrust of ideologies, collectives, and isms which characterizes Lessing's work can also be seen as a motivating factor in her biography. She repudiated her racist-colonialist homeland Africa; in her second homeland, England, she maintained a critical distance from both capitalistic and communist systems, as well as from religious and political groupings. Less-

1

ing remains an outsider on principle, in voluntary self-exile from all collectives and movements. It is this committed refusal to particularize that builds the bridge between her literary works and the stations of her biography.[2]

She was born on 22 October 1919 in Kermanshah, Persia (now Iran), the first child of British parents. Her father, Alfred Cook Tayler, born 3 August 1886 in Colchester, Essex, lived in Luton as a bank clerk until 1914, when he enlisted as a private in World War I: "I think the best of my father died in that war, that his spirit was crippled by it."[3] The war brought physical and psychological traumas for Tayler, whose leg was wounded in combat and subsequently amputated. He was nursed in the Royal Free Hospital by Sister Emily Maude McVeagh, of Irish and Scottish descent, whom he married in 1919. Lessing's mother was called by her second name, Maude, and her father by the nickname Michael.

It was typical for Michael Tayler, an idealist to a fault, to seek a new frontier after the war. Unable to face the restrictions of a bank clerk's life in England, he accepted a managerial position with the Imperial Bank of Persia. The Taylers first settled in Kermanshah, and later moved to Teheran, where Maude Tayler savored the social life of British Embassy circles.

Tayler himself was unhappy in Persia. His freedom was not substantially greater than it had been in England. On vacation in London in 1924, his interest was captured by British propaganda promising instant wealth to prospective immigrants to Southern Rhodesia. This country had been declared a self-governing colony of the British Commonwealth in 1923. The Taylers impulsively took a mortgage on a farm of three thousand acres and sailed to Africa, taking with them the relics of a more decorous life in the form of lace curtains, Persian rugs, and a piano.

The family settled near the small town of Banket in

the LoMagundi region of the Rhodesian highveld, approximately one hundred miles northwest of Salisbury (today part of Zimbabwe). The region had never before been farmed by white persons, whose number was accordingly small. Tayler, who set out to grow corn, was quickly victimized by inexperience and bad luck. Far from the fortunes promised at the Empire Exhibition in London, where maize was likened to gold, he was to scrape from one poor harvest to the next. An extremely sensitive individual to begin with, he found his dreams now finally shattered. He gradually lost his health as well as his will to overcome seemingly unsurmountable obstacles. He retreated into fantasy, superstition, and diversions such as gold prospecting (described later by his daughter in "Eldorado").

Maude Tayler, more resilient than her husband but nevertheless uprooted and lonely, met considerable difficulties trying to keep the farm going. During the entire twenty years she spent on the farm, she "waited for when life would begin," that is, for the opportunity to return to England. She became bitter and querulous and was most often at odds with her children. During World War II, her husband's health became so poor that the Taylers finally gave up the farm and moved to Salisbury, Rhodesia's capital, in 1945. Lessing's father died at the age of sixty-one three years later.

Rhodesia, the last frontier for Maude and Michael Tayler, turned out to be the decisive first frontier for their daughter. Despite the enforced isolation of farm life and chronic conflicts with her mother, certain aspects of Doris's childhood appear almost utopian. She inherited the freedom from oppressive civilization which had too long eluded her father. She spent a good part of her young years roving through the primeval veld, observing the clash between nature and incipient civilization firsthand, in the solitude which so often spawns exceptional gifts of imagination in children.

Within her family, Doris was a "rebel in residence." Her mother, while cherishing great plans for the children's education, tended to pamper them, perhaps subconsciously trying to save them for the "real life" in England to which she hoped to return. Doris lost communication with her at an early age. Her solitary hours roughing it in the bush were an antidote to the maternal pressure to be dainty and ladylike. During these years, distaste for conventional feminine roles was instilled in young Doris Tayler—an aversion the later Doris Lessing will never lose.

Her relationship with her father, on the other hand, was close and on an equal-to-equal basis. Michael Tayler always perceived his children as adults, and his daughter began to argue with him the politics of the racial situation at eight or nine years of age. She absorbed his idealism, his gift for fantasy and his sense of justice. She had at the same time to witness his painful loss of contact with reality. Her father represented to her a vulnerable individualist and idealist, broken by historical circumstance in the form of the First World War, and by his later financial struggles.

Even during her adolescence, Doris Tayler's understanding of socioeconomic conditions and their effect upon human potential was well established. At home, she watched her parents suffer the gradual depletion of their resources. They lived in rustic circumstances—in a house of mud and thatch, often improvising furniture from crates and empty gasoline drums—which would have been unthinkable in England or Persia. On the other hand, she was acutely aware that the status her family saw as degrading would still represent untold luxury to the native Rhodesians, approximately one hundred of whom were employed by her parents. This disparity can be explained by a cursory look at the structure of Rhodesian society. Statistics from the mid-1970s indicate a population amounting to six million, of

whom however only about five percent were whites of
European descent. There were nine thousand patients
per physician, a high rate of infant mortality, and 70
percent illiteracy among blacks (none among whites).
The average annual wage for a white factory worker
was $7,644, in contrast to $686 earned by an African
worker. Lessing, incensed even as a child by these inequities, was later to document statistically the African
socio-political situation in *Going Home* and in short
fictional works such as "A Home for the Highland
Cattle."

Lessing's childhood observations led not only to an
enraged compassion for the black Rhodesians, but also
to an incisive analysis of white colonialist mentality. She
developed a sixth sense for recognizing hypocrisy in the
"civilized" British at an early age. The colonial meta-
society, held together by unanimous commitment to
prolonging the subordination of the black population,
was the first concrete example of collective behavior
which Lessing came to know and instinctively hate.
Formal education was soon to become her second collective enemy. She was sent to school at the Roman
Catholic Convent in Salisbury when she was seven, an
experience she remembers as damaging. At thirteen she
transferred to the Girls' High School in the same city.
There she remained for one year during which, as she
claims, she not only learned nothing of import but was
also plagued by psychosomatic illnesses. The oft-
repeated assertion that Doris Tayler was forced to leave
school due to "eye trouble" should be taken with a grain
of salt, at the very least. She hated school and was
triumphant and relieved when the eye-trouble argument tipped the scales to her advantage in the fight
against her ambitious mother. For the next three years
she pursued an autodidactic education, reading books
ranging from Balzac, Stendhal, Dostoevsky and Tolstoy to Havelock Ellis. Structured schooling was re-

placed by her observations of highly charged racial, political, and social situations. She also collected and distilled her impressions of colonial society while living twice with families in Salisbury as an *au pair* girl.

Doris Lessing has regretted only in passing her early decision to wash her hands of formal schooling. She has often expressed her contempt for the "horse-race mentality" of educational institutions, which regard children as "commodities with a value in the success-stakes."[4] She sees modern education—far from teaching individuals to think—as a tool to mass-produce compliant citizens who will run with the herd and fit society's needs by bowing mindlessly to authority.

The farmhouse in which Doris Tayler grew up is a prototype for the important motif of rooms and houses in Lessing's work. It symbolizes the limited possibilities of separating the individual from the environment. Built upon the Taylers' arrival on the farm of logs, thatch, and mud, it was intended to tide them over a year or two until a lucrative crop would enable them to build permanently. As it turned out, they were to stay nearly twenty years. "There are two sorts of habitation in Africa. One is of brick, cement, plaster, tile and tin . . . the other sort is made direct of the stuff of soil and grass and tree. This second kind is what most of the natives of the country live in; and what I, as a child, lived in."[5] From an early age, Doris perceived the boundaries between her private life—as represented by the house—and the African landscape as permeable and fragile. The house was a temporary act of will and spite against the veld, the ants, and the climate, and was in constant danger of being swallowed by them. In one of Lessing's most memorable passages, she describes a sapling which pushed through the mud floor every rainy season, one year emerging "with a watch clutched in its leaves . . . like a Dali picture."[6] The image of the insistent sprout, handing civilization and technology back to the intruders, as it were, is a symbol for the bitter fight between the farmers and the veld. "It was the ants, of course, who finally conquered.... The rains were heavy that year, beating the house to its knees. And we heard that on the kopje there was no house, just a mound of greyish, rotting thatch, covered all over with red ant-galleries."[7]

Houses are the single image which best illustrate Lessing's distrust of partitioning and compartmentalizing. They are always depicted as vulnerable and temporary, like our efforts to encapsulate experience. Lessing puts it categorically: "For me all houses will always be wrong."[8] For they are impotent against existential homelessness, an illness of our century: "The fact is, I don't live anywhere; I never have since I left that first house on the kopje. I suspect more people are in this predicament than they know."[9]

In chronic discord with her mother, Doris Tayler left the farm in 1938 to work as a telephone operator in Salisbury. The next year she married Frank Charles Wisdom, a civil servant. She was nineteen at the time of her first marriage, which was, like her leaving school, partly an act of rebellion against parental authority. She bore a son, John, and a daughter, Jean, who were to stay in Africa when she left for England. This marriage was dissolved in 1943; thereafter she was employed briefly as a typist for a lawyer and then for a law firm. She later worked as a dictation typist for Hansard (the official Parliament Record), and on various government commissions such as the Kariba Dam project.

Between 1942 and 1948 Lessing was active in a Marxist group which was not, however, affiliated in any way with the Rhodesian Labour Party. "This was an amateur, fluxing, invented group, which no real Communist party could accept or take seriously, and as for the idea that the Labour Party could accept it . . . We were in a position—we being this heterogeneous

group of locals, refugees, airforce people—of conducting a "secret" group in full view of everyone in this small
town, and everyone knew about it, and doubtless were
waiting for us to grow up."[10] Through this group she
met Gottfried Lessing, a refugee from Hitler's Germany, whom she married in 1945. A son, Peter, her third
child, was born in 1947. The Lessings served as a focal
point for the activities of the political group, but Doris
Lessing must have realized quickly that the marriage,
like the attempt at political enlightenment in racist
Africa, was a mistake. Her second divorce in 1949 preceded her departure to England. Of marriage, against
which many of her characters rail, Lessing says, "Let's
put it this way: I do not think that marriage is one of my
talents. I've been much happier unmarried than
married."[11]

At seventeen, Lessing had written and destroyed
two entire novels and fragments of others. She began
writing at the age of nine, "poetic mush about sunsets
mostly."[12] With the modesty readers know as typical for
her, she disclaims any literary worth of her writings
prior to *The Grass is Singing*. While still in Africa, she
had submitted this novel without success to half a
dozen English publishing houses. She signed a contract
for it with a South African publisher, but when after her
arrival in England it still had not been printed, she was
advised to submit it to Michael Joseph Publishers in
London. They accepted the manuscript at once. It was
reprinted even before the official publication date and
reached seven printings within five months. This enabled
Lessing to give up a secretarial job. The successful first
novel was quickly followed by *This Was the Old
Chief's Country* (1951), *Martha Quest* (1952) and *Five*
(1953). For the latter she earned the 1954 Somerset
Maugham Award for the best work of a British author
under thirty-five. Lessing lived thenceforth exclusively
from her writing.

Despite the struggle to survive in economically ailing postwar Britain, the years after her arrival there were marked by breathtaking productivity in all literary genres. She was relieved to have escaped the oppressive Rhodesian society, where writers were constantly "in a torment of conscientiousness" over social injustice. England appeared to her in contrast as a calm haven for serious writing. There she further analyzed and increasingly rejected all forms of collective behavior. Though Marxist theory, which "looks at things as a whole and in relation to each other,"[13] provided the formative basis for Lessing's thought and works, her idealistic participation in the Rhodesian group was to remain her only wholehearted alliance with an ideologically defined collective. In England, her political activity was considerably less fervent and often concentrated on individual causes (such as circulating a petition for the Rosenbergs). Like many liberal intellectuals in the 1950s, she joined the British Communist Party, but attended meetings only sporadically; she had decided to leave it again well before she actually did so in 1956. She was also a member of a socialist writers' group, but has described herself as an "agitator manquée," whose main energy was poured onto paper rather than into active politics. Lessing disclaims any involvement with England's New Left of the 1960s, at which time she viewed all political formations with increasing distrust. Her viewpoint in 1980 is unequivocal: "Certainly I would never have anything to do with politics again unless I was forced at the point of a gun, having seen what happens."[14] All this, of course, does not change the fact that Lessing's books frequently have a politically mobilizing effect on her readers, and that her prose is at its very finest when examining the political relationship between individuals and the historical process.

Political groups are only one aspect of the *collec-*

tive, which can be defined as one of three major poles in Lessing's work. Collectivism includes nationalist affiliations, clubs of all sorts, mass support of authority and Führer-figures, and all caste or class systems. It further includes groupings determined by sex or social standing: in brief, all the structures with which individuals identify and conform in order to belong to something greater, more powerful than themselves. Collective identifications, which Lessing dissects with ever increasing acridity, are the source of lamentable human behavior: at best they produce docile and manipulable followers, at worst outbursts of mob spirit. Standing in a triad with the collective are the *individual* and the *whole*: the tension among the three runs through Lessing's work from beginning to end. Where in the early work the protagonists measure themselves against a collective standard, after *The Golden Notebook* they increasingly abandon collectives in favor of their own inner reality. Her newest, nonrealist books relegate both individuality and collectivism to second place, emphasizing instead the *whole* of nature: the organic configuration of atoms and planets which dwarfs human beings and their scrawny institutions. The holistic motif as presented in Lessing's work can lend itself to mystical, religious or back-to-nature interpretation. Of main importance is that it be distinguished from the pseudowholes presented by collectives. For where collectives level and demean individuals, Lessing sees in their linkage with the whole a possible redemption.

In the first ten years after leaving Africa, Lessing wrote four more novels, dozens of short stories, reviews, and articles, two book-length essays and three plays. In 1952 she accompanied the Authors' World Peace Appeal delegation to the Soviet Union. In the later 1950s she became involved with theater, both as an author and, as a leave replacement for Kenneth Tynan of *The Observer*, as a critic. So far she has written five plays, four of which were produced between 1958 and 1962. In addition to a translation of Alexander Ostrovsky's *The Storm* for the National Theatre, she has written four television plays (two of which are adaptations of prose works).

In 1956 Lessing traveled to South Africa and Rhodesia, where she had in the meantime been declared a "prohibited immigrant" because of her Communist affiliation and unconcealed criticism of the white-supremacist regime. She was never officially informed that she was "prohibited." In 1953 Southern Rhodesia, Northern Rhodesia, and Nyasaland had been linked by Britain into a Federation, which was dissolved in 1964. Lessing's trip thus came at a time of temporary and fragile political equilibrium: she was among the first to diagnose that the Federation was not working. Her account of this journey is found in *Going Home* (1957), her major journalistic work. Lessing was not to return to Africa again until over twenty-five years later, in the summer of 1982.

While the early books received consistent and emphatic acclaim, it was *The Golden Notebook* in 1962 that really brought Lessing international prominence. It is generally considered to be her finest achievement. New translations of this novel invariably touch off an explosion of interest in her works— as demonstrated in eight non-English-speaking countries to date. The novel was instrumental in establishing her reputation in Western Europe. Since its publication in Germany in 1978, she has held an active place in the West German literary forum, and received two literary prizes from German-speaking countries in 1982.

The Golden Notebook is a sweeping examination of an individual's final reckoning with many collectives, ranging from communism to feminism. Its viewpoint is that of disillusionment: with the socialist dream, with the hope for a better world, and with traditional femi-

ninity. Feminists in English-speaking countries (who
are, ironically, one of the collectives whose *causa* is
partially invalidated by the book), immediately adopted
the novel as a spearhead for the movement. Lessing
herself has adamantly refused to take sides in the war
between the sexes, which, as she correctly diagnoses,
often serves as a modish substitute for serious class
conflict: "I say we should all go to bed, shut up about
sexual liberation, and go on with the important matters."[15] Nevertheless, the book set a milestone in British
literature through its uninhibited depiction of female
sexuality. It continued to be a favorite of feminist readers throughout the 1970s, since it formulates so potently
many of the movement's arguments. (A good many of
them, in fact, can already be found in *A Proper Marriage*, published in 1954.) Its undiminished popularity
with an increasingly political feminist movement provides proof of the author's own premise: that there can
be no women's cause independent of humanity's social
and political causes on the whole front. *The Golden
Notebook* must be seen as a first zenith of Lessing's
work, which in 1962 was only at the beginning of its
multifaceted and unpredictable development.

In 1964, Lessing reviewed *The Sufis* by Idries Shah,
the chief proponent of modern Sufism. Using her usual
autodidactic method, she immersed herself in reading
about Sufism throughout the 1960s. Since that time,
many critics have investigated Sufi mysticism as a key
to understanding Lessing's work, especially the two last
volumes of *Children of Violence*.[16] Though mysticism
undoubtedly plays a role in the development of Lessing's thought, it is important to keep it in perspective.
Doris Lessing is not an esoteric writer, and it is perfectly
possible to appreciate and interpret her novels without
deeper knowledge of Sufism—which is, after all, still an
ism. The school of belief is over a thousand years old,
and differs from similar religious and mystic groups in

that there is no official hierarchy. Any person in any walk of life can be "a Sufi." This is a crucial point: Lessing would never subscribe to a doctrine dependent on gurus and authority figures. Sufism emphasizes the individual expansion of consciousness and, concurrently, repudiation of propaganda, ideology, and prejudice: "Sufism believes itself to be the substance of that current which can develop man to a higher stage in his evolution."[17] Sufi mysticism transcends national, religious, material and racial boundaries and encourages individuals to recognize their importance to the greater scheme of the human race. Clearly, this canon did not revolutionize Lessing's thinking, but rather reinforced insights which were present from the beginning: "I became interested in the Sufi way of thought because I was already thinking like that, before I had heard of Sufis or Sufism. My most 'Sufi' book was the *Golden Notebook*, written before I had heard of mysticism."[18]

The Four-Gated City, published in 1969, represents a major turning point in Lessing's production. It is the fifth and last volume of the sequence *Children of Violence*, which was begun in 1951 as an exhaustive exploration of our century's "whole pattern of discrimination and tyranny and violence" as it affects one heroine, Martha Quest. While the first four volumes depict her grappling with various collectives, the fifth book breaks up this polarity, which appears petty and confining once Martha envisions the "whole" spectrum of human experience. She discovers the subconscious, the extrasensory and the "mad" parts of her consciousness. The book transcends the previous realist boundaries of Lessing's narrative scope; by abandoning an empirical time framework it ends around the year 2000. This is a first in Lessing's oeuvre, and probably the most crucial step in the development of her vision away from individual-bound realism and toward holistic fantasies.

On the basis of both *The Four-Gated City* and

Briefing For a Descent Into Hell (1971), many of Lessing's critics connected her works to those of the popular British psychiatrist R. D. Laing. Though she is familiar with his writings, she was already deeply involved with her own assessment of madness before reading Laing's *The Divided Self* (1959). Laing was only one of a host of psychologists and sociologists, among them Erich Fromm, who concluded in the late fifties that psychoanalysis is often used to stifle individuality, to force the patient to conform to the "normal" standards of a sick society. A more fruitful comparison would be that of Lessing's work to the documentation on schizophrenia by Bert Kaplan,[19] which she read in the late 1960s. But the insight which links her to this school of thought—that insanity is in fact a rational reaction to a violent society—can be traced back to the first decade of her literary work.

In 1969 Lessing toured the United States. In keeping with her aversion to formal education, she refused to give lectures, but conducted question-and-answer sessions on college campuses, which allowed her to speak directly to audiences. Her trip coincided with the peak of student protests against the Vietnam War, and the concomitant peace movement. Ironically, while she was greeted by older readers with acclaim and admiration, many students were too busy agitating to take part in the seminars. Shocked by the arrest of demonstrators, she encouraged protestors to organize against the threat of a totalitarian state: "while you can act openly, you should act openly, and fight for the right to act openly."[20]

Lessing's interest in the United States' powerful influence on modern history goes back to the mid-1950s. In the wake of the 1956 Soviet invasion of Hungary, she not only formally withdrew from the Communist party, but at the same time sharpened her critical awareness of the USA with its distressing similarities to South Africa.[21] Her observations were supported by the excesses of the McCarthy era, during which the Republican senator Joseph R. McCarthy of Wisconsin led witch-hunts against scores of alleged Communists and subversives. The events of 1950-1955 struck fear and trembling into Americans, who saw that their own government could turn against them; and indirectly into the British, who feared for their civil liberties as well. In New York in 1969, Lessing remembers, "In the USA radicals haven't had an easy time. McCarthyism has had a long-term effect on this country and on England, and it hasn't been measured. A great many American friends of mine were destroyed by McCarthy. . . . It's a good thing that young people have escaped that atmosphere. They are freer and braver, but they should realize that McCarthyism can reappear."[22] Lessing made a second trip to the United States in 1974, at which time she was awarded honorary memberships in the American Academy of Arts and Letters, the Institute for Cultural Research, and the Modern Language Association.

While Lessing has always worked to enlighten, sensitize, and edify, her belief in the possible betterment of humanity's situation has consistently dwindled. Where she once insisted that black and white, East and West could coexist if only true human contact were established, she has long come to view the catastrophic self-annihilation of civilization, looming since the cold war, as inevitable. Even without the atom bomb, humanity's chances of feeding and clothing, much less educating itself, are slim. Of a world in which 42,000 children per day die of malnutrition and disease (United Nations/World Health Organization Statistics for 1982), Lessing says, "This is the apocalypse, here and now."[23]

Another phase of prolific production in the early 1970s attests to the author's growing pessimism. She released three novels within four years: *Briefing For a*

Descent Into Hell was followed by *The Summer Before the Dark* (1973) and *The Memoirs of a Survivor* (1974). The books explore "inner space": their protagonists retreat into the realm of the subconscious in search of meaning after their external, collective identifications break down. Though the heroes' "madness" is shown as a viable response to society's demands, the first two ultimately resume their "sane" roles, and the third novel suspends rather than solves the conflict through a mystical vision.

After *Memoirs*, Lessing shifts her focus from individual madness and collective doom toward that "whole" of humanity glimpsed in *The Four-Gated City*. Ending a lull of nearly five years, she embarked in 1979 on an unprecedented novel series, *Canopus in Argos: Archives*. Once again, the novels attest to furious productivity—at the time of this writing, five volumes have been published in less than four years. Lessing now abandons realism to invent a counteruniverse, in which individuals are not plagued by the illusion of free will, and collective action appears as a mere Band-Aid on civilization's festering wounds. Wholeness, on the other hand, can be envisioned and even put to paper, as Canopus's industrious archivists prove. With this series, it is necessary to draw an unavoidably simplistic line between the "old," realist Lessing, and the "new" Lessing. Most of her readers clearly identify with one or the other. Where older readers are often perplexed and disappointed by the new books, many under thirty are enthusiastic, and dismiss the 1960s realism of *The Golden Notebook* or the no-exit racial and social dilemmas of *The Grass is Singing* as boring and depressing.

Doris Lessing lives inconspicuously in a house in London. She seldom gives interviews, but corresponds generously with readers and critics. In explanation of her productivity, which has continued untiringly for over thirty years, she admits that she writes very fast, drawing from inspiration rather than calculation: "I share with D. H. Lawrence the belief that often it is the first writing that has the vitality. If you mess about and tinker with a thing, it loses freshness."[24] She also emphasizes her reliance on the subconscious, which she allows to surface through slumber: "When I'm stuck in a book I deliberately dream. . . . I fill my brain with the material for a new book, go to sleep, and I usually come up with a dream which resolves the dilemma."[25] No doubt her unconventional methods contribute to the superior momentum of her prose, but also to a reckless style which is frequently criticized as careless and gangling. Paradoxically, the reader is often confronted with ungrammatical sentences oblivious to words like "whom," full of badly placed commas and relative pronouns—but whose substance is singularly well-put and persuasive.

Lessing's influence and popularity have increased steadily since the publication of her first novel. Her works have always provoked vehement reactions: she has been scorned as a communist and as a traitor to communism; labeled a radical, a feminist, a liberal. She has the distinction of being banned from certain bookstore shelves as "not decent."[26] In fact, most of her work up to 1974 is traditional in style and theme, designed to communicate with a large readership through its feet-on-the-ground diagnosis of the human situation. The "radicalism" of her realist works lies only in their insistence on calling things by their right names. The newer books, despite their intergalactic perspective, still have as their main subject the exploration of social and psychological processes, and are designed to deepen the reader's concept of self in relation to the universe.

Lessing's novels have been translated into more than twenty languages and are read the world over. She received the French Prix Medici for foreign literature in 1976 and, in 1982, both the German Shakespeare Prize and the Austrian State Prize for European Literature.

Over thirty-five dissertations have been done on her books, several of them published, and many more are in the making. The Modern Language Association of America has devoted an annual seminar to Lessing since 1971, and the formation of the Doris Lessing Society in the United States led to the publication of the *Doris Lessing Newsletter*, a journal founded in 1976 and at this writing entering its eighth year. Of course, these distinctions only attest to the fact that Lessing's attack on particularism has been unsuccessful on the whole. For she includes herself and her works in the maxim that no individual compartment of human life is of solitary importance. Lessing disdains clubs, including the ones devoted to her, and wants to avoid becoming a cult figure or mascot. The reader who perceives Lessing's works as they are intended will avoid coquettish labels such as "Dorisologist" or "Lessing Freak,"[27] and keep a critical distance to collectives and clubs. In the preface to *The Golden Notebook* Lessing cautions the devotee of her works: "Dear Student. You are mad. Why spend months and years writing thousands of words about one book, or even one writer, when there are hundreds of books waiting to be read. You don't see that you are the victim of a pernicious system.... Why are [critics] so parochial, so personal, so small-minded? Why do they always atomise, and belittle, why are they so fascinated by detail, and uninterested in the whole?"[28] But it is often the interest in the "whole" which leads readers to Doris Lessing's books, in search of a deeper awareness of their time. Most will agree that a close reading of Lessing helps dispel parochialism and leads to a greater, more valid picture of ourselves, our fellow beings, and our place in history. Reading Lessing "enlarges our perception of life," and it is my hope that this book will provide some guidelines for a perceptive approach to her works.

2

A Splendid Backdrop
to a Disgraceful Scene:
African Fiction 1950-1965

The Grass is Singing

Three years before Lessing moved to England, bring-
ing with her the already oft-rejected *Grass is Singing*,
she had given up a position with a legal firm in Salisbury
to begin writing it. Though she had at that point already
published various short prose and poetic texts, the tack-
ling of a longer fictional work was a sink-or-swim test of
her conviction that she would "some day" become a
professional writer. The theme for the first novel
resulted directly from her observation of the color conflict that was a matter of course in her African surroundings: "I had kept a newspaper cutting about a black man
murdering a white woman. No motive! I had spent
years wondering why black servants did not murder
neurotic, nagging, contemptuous housewives. Soon I
was able to see those women as pathetic."[1]

The success of Lessing's first book was facilitated
by the British literary climate around 1950. Novels,
especially nonexperimental ones, were in great demand,
and the English readership was constantly on the look-
out for new talents. Accordingly, many young writers
were able to make a breakthrough with a first novel and
to establish a circle of readers who would remain faithful for years to come. This was precisely Lessing's situation. A second factor in her favor was the book's subject

matter: it attracted the typically British interest in class
structures, social hierarchies, and abused mores. The
Rhodesian setting further guaranteed the novel's appeal
to readers of a long tradition of colonial literature, all
the more so since most British knew relatively little
about this colony, which did not make headlines until
the 1960s. Lessing's was the first book on the British
literary scene to take on the theme that a few years later
would be in full vogue and even scorned as "the colour
bore."[2]

Regular reprintings of *The Grass is Singing*
throughout the 1960s and 1970s have made it one of
Lessing's best-read titles. It not only avoids many of the
pitfalls typical of first novels, it also foreshadows most
of the strengths—the style, the dominant themes and
incisive realism—of the works to follow in the coming
decades. Lessing's first novel is a study of the individual
both outcast and self-exiled from the ruling collective.
It not only laments the protagonist's stunted vision, but
also rides a sharp attack on collective behavior, which
welcomes the pariah's demise and insists on the division
of society into black and white.

The book opens with a newspaper clipping report-
ing the murder of Mary Turner by a black servant. The
somber ending is known to the reader from the outset,
adding to the undercurrent of inevitability ever-present
in the narrative tone. A lengthy flashback traces Mary's
bleak childhood, spent in station towns under the
shadow of a tyrannical alcoholic father and a battered
mother. The first decisive turn in Mary's life is her
enrollment in boarding school, which she views as paradise compared to home. After her parents' death, she
remains in a prolonged childhood, living in a "Girls
Club" until she is over thirty. She then gives in to society's customary pressure to wed, and impulsively marries Dick Turner, a farmer: "It might have been anybody".(44)[3] This is the second major event in her life

and the turning point that initiates her irreversible decline. Brought by Dick, still a near-stranger, to a desolate and poverty-stricken shack overlooking ill-fated farmlands, her initial resourcefulness and determination are gradually depleted. Her one attempt to return to town is foiled, as is her endeavor to save the farm from Dick's mismanagement.

The wasteland of infertile fields mirrors the lack of intimacy between Dick and Mary Turner, who are held together by circumstance and mutual pity. While Dick exhausts himself through fanatic overwork on the fields, Mary turns inward to a private world much more complex than her husband's. She gradually loses her mental equilibrium and sinks into apathy, which is disrupted only by her animosity toward the black workers. The final blow to Mary's physical and mental breakdown is dealt by her love-hate relationship with a virile and intelligent servant, Moses. At first fascinated, then obsessed with him, she slips into an equivocal vise of emotional dependence and mortal fear. In an hysterical attempt to regain control and to save face before the farming assistant Marston, who has observed her with Moses, she bans Moses from the house. This, her last deliberate action, at once seals her fate, for she knows he will kill her for her betrayal, and in the last night before the Turners were to leave the farm, she goes to the verandah to wait for death. When Moses appears with a knife and kills her "with the satisfaction of his completed revenge," the book's action has come full circle.

The Grass is Singing is sustained by two distinct but inseparable currents: the tragic disintegration of Mary Turner's personality on one hand, and omnipresent racial tension on the other. Though some critics have lamented the fact that "Lessing's passion against racial prejudice causes her to disrupt her main concern [with Mary's mental degeneration],"[4] the two themes cannot

be severed. In fact, their entwinement lays a corner-
stone for all of Lessing's early works, in which personal
development is always propelled and determined by
the greater social framework. The first chapter illustrates that framework through the viewpoint of an outsider, Marston (whose story was developed at length in
Lessing's early drafts of the novel), as well as through an
omniscient analysis of the white Rhodesian community
and its reaction to the murder. Despite the chronic
hunger for gossip, this case is veiled in taboo. Every-
body seems to have hated Mary, and all are relieved by
the murder which, though they are unsure of its motivation, undoubtedly "served her right." It is important
that Mary Turner as protagonist is introduced only *after*
a detailed sketch of the small-minded collective—ruled
by opportunism, racism, and intolerance—from which
she was an outcast. From the very beginning, this individual is portrayed in the context of her social environment. The young Lessing does not beat about the bush,
but moves straight to the subject of her critical focus—
the collective—in the novel's exposition.

Accordingly, Lessing shows that the seeds of
Mary's demise are planted by circumstance long before
she comes to the farm. She grows up in the squalid
setting of her parents' degrading marriage. Filled with
revulsion for her father and used as a confidante by her
embittered mother, she is emotionally crippled at an
early age. She is unable to adopt an adult female role
and remains emotionally adolescent for fifteen years.
Lessing's early figures react to society's pressures in two
typical ways—total conformity or total evasion. Mary
chooses the latter route, hoping through her initial
repudiation of marriage and sexuality to escape the
abysmal misery she saw her parents endure. As a substitute for heterosexual relationships, she surrounds herself with casual acquaintances and often sinks into the
world of illusion offered by movies and cheap novels.

Even stronger than her decision to evade adulthood, however, is her compulsion to be considered normal by society's standards. And "normal" women observe the mandate of the Rhodesian social hierarchy requiring them to marry. Mary has not only neglected to do so, but has also naively continued to consider herself ordinary, and is thus horrified to overhear a remark implying that she is sexually abnormal ("She's not like that"). This remark motivates all that follows, and is to haunt her until her death.

Mary Turner is the first victim of what Lessing's critics call "fragmented vision," a trait common to many of her female figures. She perceives her surroundings through a mental prism and cannot synthesize the refracted segments of her experience into a meaningful whole. She discerns individual aspects (a houseboy, a disparaging remark) without the perspective of a greater context (class conflicts, suppressed sexuality). These fragmented perceptions leave her confused, and motivated by fear rather than conviction. Thus her prolonged single status, which, as the narrator points out, grants her privileges for which ideology-bound feminists in other societies do hard battle, is strictly the result of subconscious aversion and anxiety. Equally, her eventual marriage is motivated by her fear of society's verdict, when it becomes stronger than her fear of matrimony. Mary's inability to recognize, much less analyze, the full spectrum of forces that motivate her paves the way for the later disintegration of her sanity.

Where she once hoped to save herself from marriage, she now expects marriage to save her from herself. Lessing's assessment of this institution is already well formed here. At best, it intensifies individual weakness rather than alleviating it; at worst, it is the ticket for a descent into hell. This particular marriage is based on the self-delusions of both parties. Dick, driven by loneliness, conjures up a haunting sylph who has little to do

with the real Mary. She, on the other hand, allows her
all-too-realistic memories of her parents' marriage to be
dimmed by social pressure: "She felt vaguely that she
had been right to marry—everyone had been right"
(53). This briefly satisfying identification with the collective quorum "everyone" is soon annulled by the realities of her husband, who is weak, self-abasing, and
masochistic. Though external hardship brings Dick and
Mary closer together, they never establish lasting contact. She despises him and is repulsed by his physical
presence, and the two enter a kind of solitary confine-
ment *à deux*, locked in loneliness that further contributes to their decline.

Mary and Dick Turner represent the two irreconcilable opposites in Lessing's work: "the city and the
veld,"[5] or civilization and nature. The mutual attraction
and repulsion of these two forces produces a dynamic
tension which flows through most of Lessing's works.
Mary loves crowds, hot running water, and paved
walkways. Dick, in contrast, is plagued by claustro-
phobia, which swells to murderous proportions when
he is in town and is assuaged only by the endless
expanses of empty bush. Concurrent with her love of
civilization's comforts, Mary is disgusted by untamed
nature and, particularly, by sexuality. On her wedding
night, she sublimates her revulsion into apathy: "It was
not so bad, she thought, when it was all over: not as bad
as *that*. It meant nothing to her, nothing at all. Expecting
outrage and imposition, she was relieved to find she felt
nothing" (57). Her first hours on the farm, however, are
already filled with foreboding: she sees herself about to
trace her mother's pitiful footsteps, and she automati-
cally transfers her hatred of her father to Dick. Given to
superstition rather than analysis, she broods on "the
thought that her father, from his grave, had sent out his
will and forced her back into the kind of life he had
made her mother lead" (56). For Mary, as for many of

Lessing's figures, life's biggest crisis comes with the realization that she is in danger of repeating her parents' mistakes, no matter how hard she tries to avoid them. When she fails to change course *despite* this insight, her fate is sealed. Her fear of repetition is ultimately less powerful than her fear of straying from the path circumstance seems to have chosen for her.

While psychological factors are important in the process of Mary's decline, its speed and extent are determined by poverty. Lessing draws a clear parallel between economic stress and the endangered personality: it is this mutual illumination of emotional and economic plights that sets the author off from nearly all of her contemporaries from the beginning of her career. In this novel, the Turners' destitution is symbolized by the missing ceilings which could have cooled the sweltering hut in which Mary feels incarcerated. Poverty is an inferno which gnaws continually on her reserves of hope and strength. Confronted with the now inevitable alienation and drudgery of married life, Mary's instinctive reaction is hostility toward the native servants. At first glance, her otherwise introverted passivity contradicts the tyrannical energy she summons when dealing with her houseboys. On closer scrutiny, however, her behavior is as logical as the proverbial kicking of the dog. Both her Rhodesian background and her limited vision bind her to observance of the ruling vertical hierarchical structures. She is unable to channel her aggressions upward, challenging the oppressive social mores which ruined her parents and in turn crippled her own capacity for human contact. As a woman in a patriarchal society, she cannot openly turn against her husband. Instead, she strikes out at her fellow-oppressed, the natives—the only beings she feels to be lowlier than herself. Her relationship to Moses is a battle for the illusion of power between the powerless and oppressed, with which Lessing also establishes the analogous status

of females and blacks as backed up by historical examples.[6] Both are outcasts in a segregated, group-oriented
society and, since neither has hope of challenging the
dominant collective, they instead turn against each
other.

Mary hates the native Africans for their "stoical
apathy," which perfectly describes her own condition,
and is particularly nauseated by their spontaneous and
sparsely clothed sexuality. The experience of bullying
them is exhilarating for her, since it gives her the illusion
of strength and control. At the same time, however,
Mary depends on the workers for companionship.
Moses is the only human being in Mary's private wasteland, his kindness her last tie with life as she loses
contact with reality and her mind becomes a "soft ach-
ing blank." She is first bound to him by morbid fascina-
tion, since he exhibits all the qualities she lacks: strength,
determination, sexual potency, indifference to abuse.[7]
In order to keep Moses, she relinquishes her listless
frigidity and becomes, in a grotesque reversal, "like
that"—hysterically flirtatious and giddily feminine.
This by day—at night she is paralyzed by fear.

Lessing's efforts to penetrate the character of
Moses are not entirely successful; in this respect, the
compact volume bites off more than it can chew.[8] He
appears, behind the mask of subservient kindness, to be
motivated by the intense satisfaction of manipulating
and humiliating Mary. But more important than his
contribution to her downfall is Moses's function as a
symbol for the potential of black Africa. He clearly
stands for the superiority of other races over the Anglo-
Saxons. His powerful, almost superhuman physique
effectively dwarfs everyone near him. Mary, who despises sexuality, is mesmerized by his virility: "She used
to sit quite still, watching him work. The powerful,
broad-built body fascinated her . . . his muscles bulged
and filled out the thin material of the sleeves until it

seemed they would split" (164). While the white settler
Dick Turner atrophies in Africa, the "subordinate"
black of course flourishes. He possesses not only physical prowess, but also limitless reserves of patience and
self-discipline, qualities which elude the whites to a
great extent. If not logically compelling, Moses's revenge
appears at least symbolically valid. He has commanded
Mary to keep him in her house and in fact deposed her
from authority. When she suddenly reverts to her previous dominant position—as white mistress—his revenge is inevitable. The analogy to greater color conflict is clear. Moses's moment of triumph over his
oppressors is worth his life to him: just as in the history
of South Africa, which is implied here, no number of
deaths will be able to impede the slow reacquisition of
the continent by the Africans.

At the end of the book, we know why it is Mary
Turner's crime and not Moses's that incenses the dis-
trict. She has betrayed her color-coded status by
depending on a native, and is thus beyond redemption.
Even the physical manifestations of such a transgression are intolerable, as shown by the reaction of a
neighbor, Charlie Slatter, to the Turners' use of brightly
colored native cloth ("kaffir truck"). He is revolted by
this violation of "the first law of white South Africa,
which is: 'Thou shalt not let your fellow whites sink
lower than a certain point; because if you do, the nigger
will see he is as good as you are'" (210). Needless to say,
Mary's breach of the color bar on a human, emotional
level is an unspeakable delict; and the white collective,
feeling it owes her no more allegiance, sees the death
penalty imposed on her as just.

Paradoxically, her last helpless outburst against
Moses, which seals her death, is made to preserve
appearances before Marston, who, as an outsider, is
puzzled but certainly not shocked by the scene he has
observed. From his viewpoint, it need never have been

censured, much less have led to Mary's murder. Only
within the stringent Rhodesian social code is the tragic
ending inevitable. But Mary is unable to align the fragments of her perception with any redeeming outside
viewpoint. She remains uncomprehending and resigned
to her death: "I don't understand, she said again. I
understand nothing. The evil is there, but of what it
consists, I do not know ... [this night] would finish her.
And justly—she knew that. But why? Against what had
she sinned?" (230). Implicit in Mary's fatal "cracked
vision" is Lessing's appeal to the individual to maintain
intact perception, to repudiate the collective forces of
political and personal oppression, and not merely to
turn against fellow victims.

The narrator observes that Mary often "did the
right thing, but for the wrong reasons." Had she defied
society's oppressive institutions out of conviction, rather
than of fear and neurosis, she might not have lost her
hold on life. A more constructive defiance of the same
society will be the task of a stronger heroine in the
Martha Quest novels. *The Grass is Singing*, its title taken
from T. S. Eliot's poem cycle *The Waste Land*,[9] provides a moving analysis of socioeconomic circumstance
as it weakens and finally destroys the individual. At the
same time, the portrayal of the heroine sheds a striking
critical light on a collectivistic society: "It is by the
failures and misfits of a civilization that one can best
judge its weaknesses."[10]

African Stories

Lessing's second book publication was a collection
of ten short stories set in Africa: *This Was the Old
Chief's Country* (1951). Two years later she published
the five short novels of *Five* (1953): "A Home for the
Highland Cattle," "Eldorado," "The Antheap," "Hun-

ger," and "The Other Woman," of which only the last uses a British setting. In all, Lessing has written over thirty short prose texts set in South Africa. These impress the reader as a multifaceted and richly detailed extension of the scenery that *The Grass is Singing* restricted to one fated farm. Taken as a whole, they are probably Lessing's most enticingly readable cycle. Undeniably, her African experiences, poured into the dynamic short-story genre, provided an ideal basis for the development of her narrative talent. The African stories seem to surge out of a single creative impulse, sustained by Lessing's infectious enthusiasm for the landscape that frames the violent collisions of life and death, black and white, civilization and nature.

These stories shape and temper the narrative techniques that are to remain more or less predominant in her work. Her observations are both graphic and instinctively accurate; the perspective usually omniscient. Lessing's narrative approach here is traditional and has often been called anachronistic: her autodidactic training in nineteenth-century fiction by Balzac, Tolstoy, Dostoevsky, Stendhal, Gogol and others left her remarkably immune to the stylistic innovations of twentieth-century British literature (i.e., James Joyce or Virginia Woolf, to name only two).[11] Just as Lessing's universal themes appeal to a broad readership, she avoids artificial or experimental barriers between the narrator and the reader.

If one seeks a common denominator in all thirty African stories, it lies in the theme of the individual's collision with an oppressive environment. While the young may emerge temporarily unscathed from this skirmish, the adults, whose strength is already eroded by poverty and hardship, are nearly always doomed. Lessing's masterful short stories entwine the social upheavals in twentieth-century Africa with individual fates and achieve a gripping diagnosis of the evils of our

time: oppression, racism, isolation, poverty, intolerance, aggression. Underlying all this is the author's love
of Africa and her firm belief in its limitless potential:
thus do the stories evoke a "splendid backdrop to a
disgraceful scene"—the scene of oppressed humanity.[12]

The themes of *The Grass is Singing* are closely
paralleled in "The Second Hut." Again the setting is a
doomed farm, run by the British immigrant Major Carruthers, whose wife has become an invalid through
"heart-break over the conditions they lived in." The
story develops a triangle consisting of Carruthers, his
native employees, and the Dutch assistant Van Heerden.
All three belong to groups crippled by socioeconomic
circumstance. The malnourished natives live in squalor.
The British immigrant is broken by debt and farming
failures. Van Heerden, finally, represents the Afrika-
ners or Boers, Dutch settlers who were decimated by
the British in the Boer War (1899-1902) and thereafter
often descended into the despised class of the "poor
white." The time is 1931, and severe depression has left
thousands of Boers unemployed. Van Heerden comes
to Carruthers after he has spent three-fourths of a year
camping with his wife and nine children on the veld.

Poverty is the moving force in this constellation of
oppressed groups. It makes the three proponents of the
triangle (who, for historical reasons, are irreconcilable
enemies) dependent on each other, since Carruthers
needs workers and an assistant, and these in turn need
employment. But their tenuous truce is upset when
Carruthers imposes on his native workers, whom Van
Heerden maltreats, to build a larger hut for the Boer
family. This they do, only to burn it down again soon,
fatally burning the youngest Boer child. The natives
join forces with the elements, in the form of fire, to
express their collective hatred of the Boers; Van
Heerden, in turn, has also observed the tradition of
animosity and accepts their revenge as its natural con-

sequence. He further accepts the child's death without great ado—it is soon to be replaced by a premature tenth baby. But Carruthers, whose initiative brings such catastrophic results, realizes to what dire extent the combined factors of collective hatred and poverty can undermine the ethical sense in human beings. Rather than risk this kind of moral decay, he capitulates and plans his return to England. The story's essence is comparable to that of the first novel. The individual's hopeless struggle against his surroundings is determined first by poverty, then by a transgression against the social code. Already weakened by economic circumstance, Carruthers seals his fate when he forcefully disrupts the hierarchy of the oppressed by trying to better the position of one pole (the Dutch) through the goodwill of the other (the natives).

This confining social nexus plays a decisive part in many of the stories. It demands respect for the mechanisms of oppression, observance of the color bar, and conformity to role stereotypes. Lessing often analyzes this setting through the experience of female figures, who are particularly susceptible to the pressures of the power hierarchy. A good example is found in Molly Slatter of "Getting Off the Altitude." Molly reacts to loneliness and hardship by observing a traditionally feminine role, complete with the womanly qualities of self-abnegation, vulnerability, and subservience. She submits, ladylike and helpless, to the bullying of a contemptuous husband. Molly, like Mary Turner or the heroine of "Lucy Grange," is unable to fight against oppression and isolation. These women "learn to accept the second-rate" and grasp at any shred of human contact: Mary at Moses, Lucy Grange at a traveling salesman, Molly at the sexual attentions of the farming assistant. Ironically, all three women seek solace by entering an exploitive relationship which further entrenches their role of feminine acquiescence. Molly

Slatter escapes Mary Turner's tragic end, since she does
not cross the color bar. But she fervently curses (over-
heard only by the narrator) both sexuality and her feminine role, and pins her meager hopes on approaching
old age, which will release her from the strictures of
both.

Characteristically, the figures of the African stories
respond to their solitude through heightened sensuality.
In "Getting Off the Altitude," it is sublimated through
slavish observance of traditional sex roles. In other stories, it gives rise to unconventional sexual attractions,
which may take extreme forms (such as the insanity of
the protagonist in "Plants and Girls") or, more often, run
in subtle undercurrents: between a middle-aged farmer
and a young girl ("The New Man"), or between two
brothers who share one wife ("Winter in July"). This
story's heroine, Julia, maintains intact vision, as opposed
to Mary Turner. She remains intellectually in control of
the situation, if unable to change it. She is comparable in
this respect to Mrs. Gale of "The De Wets Come to
Kloof Grange." These two stories build a direct bridge
to the feminist themes of Lessing's later works, address-
ing the situation of a self-aware woman "facing the
sorrowful abdication of middle age" (246) in a male-
dominated world. "Winter in July" is one of the rare
African stories whose characters reject collective identity stereotypes and in fact gain insight into their plight.
It thereby reinforces Lessing's thesis, which will be
expanded in the *Children of Violence* novels, that an
analytical and individual grasp on one's situation is the
first step toward lessening its indignities.

Concurrent with the depiction of the doomed British, whose fight against poverty and loneliness is usually
futile, a number of stories revolve around the natural
superiority and tenacity of the native Africans. While
they are to a certain extent corruptible by white society
("Hunger" or "A Home for the Highland Cattle"), they

possess natural dignity ("Old Chief Mshlanga") and an innate resilience most whites will never attain. This is triumphantly demonstrated in "No Witchcraft for Sale," in which white medical science proves no match for tribal sorcery. The African is also vastly unscrupulous in gaining revenge ("The Pig," "The Nuisance"). This vengefulness cannot be quelled even by the most benevolent white settlers ("Little Tembi"). The color-bar power structure finds its most resonant expression in "The Black Madonna," which Lessing describes in the preface as "full of the bile that in fact I feel for the 'white' society in Southern Rhodesia as I knew and hated it" (p. x).

"The Antheap" poignantly develops the antithesis of white and black, and postulates a synthesis of the two forces symbolized by a mulatto child. The story is again supported by a triangle, consisting of the white boy, Tommy; the miner, Mr. Macintosh (who embodies exploitative white supremacy); and Dirk, his unacknowledged child by a native woman. Tommy recognizes that Dirk deserves an education, which he is determined to ensure even at the expense of his own schooling. This text exhibits some of Lessing's most compelling imagery. Tommy, whose youthful sense of justice is yet intact, respects the natural superiority of the Africans. This is symbolized by his carved likeness of Dirk's (black) mother. He chooses the hardest indigenous wood available, that of the thorn tree, which immediately blunts his knife: "a close-fibred, knotted wood, and down its centre, as he knew, was a hard black spine" (400). His first likeness of Dirk is modeled of clay: a substance infinitely more malleable than the hardwood representing the older generation. The clay represents the strength of the African soil itself. Some years later, Tommy carves a second statue of his friend from a tree trunk which he leaves rooted—indeed the roots, a symbol of Dirk's inviolable bond with the African continent, provide the focal point of the carving. Tommy's aesthetic vision is undaunted by Macintosh's argument that the roots are rotten and will be devoured by ants in any event.

Not surprisingly, it is by violence, again in the form of fire, that Macintosh hopes to foil Tommy's secret education of his friend. He burns down the hideout in which Dirk has hidden and studied Tommy's smuggled schoolbooks. Though eventually he capitulates and agrees to send Dirk to the university, he does so not for the sake of Dirk's talents but because he is afraid of losing the white boy, who is dear to him. His loyalty to the white collective is unshakable—accordingly, he does not attain a more mature vision, but instead is "defeated by something he did not begin to understand" (423).

That Tommy is able to bridge the color bar, where Carruthers of "The Second Hut" failed, can be attributed to the factor of his youth: the single stronghold of hope in these texts. Many of the African stories are told through the vigorous viewpoint of the white child, who is at one with the teeming veld and nature itself. The child's eyes focus on three major subject groups: the color bar and native custom, the social hierarchy among the settlers and, most important, the basic workings of life and death within unadulterated nature. Of the last group, "The Story of Two Dogs," "The Sun Between Their Feet," and "Sunrise on the Veld" are the most memorable.

"Sunrise on the Veld" establishes an intrinsic tie between a fifteen-year-old boy and the entire African landscape, through which he roams in the early morning hours. It traces the boy's three steps toward mature vision, expressed by the symmetrically placed words "eternity," "fatality," and "responsibility." The first section is devoted to the boy's exultant sense of power as he bounds over the waking veld. The sight of a buck being eaten alive by ants fills him with a distinct sense of fatality: "If I had not come it would have died like this: so why should I interfere? . . . this is what happens, this is how things work . . . *it was right and nothing could alter it*" (66; emph. orig.). Only on closer inspection of the animal's soon clean-picked carcass, whose broken leg bone must have prevented its escape from the ants, does it dawn on the boy that he himself took a potshot at just such a young buck some mornings past. He realizes that, in his drunken joy of life, he must have inflicted the wound that predetermined a painful death. In short, Lessing draws a thumbnail sketch of the cycle of life, suffering and death, and hinges the whole picture on the consciousness of one adolescent: who may or may not, in time, rework the incident into ethical conviction.

The child on the veld represents the yet-intact bond between human beings and nature, an ideal aspired to by most of Lessing's characters. This perspective is complemented by that of children who observe adult society from the fringes, narrating with the heightened sensibility of adolescence ("Old John's Place," "The New Man," "Getting Off the Altitude"). These child narrators are still suspended between nature and society, aware of the conflicts and injustices involved in adult life, but not yet bent into conformity. As we know from *The Grass is Singing*, whose protagonist goes directly from pink-pinafored childhood into oppressed middle age, this state of innocence is tenuous, the step into downtrodden adulthood swift and inevitable.

Lessing's African stories are among modern literature's most compelling delineations of individual fate against the tableau of historical circumstance. It is their rare achievement to show the individual "as a microcosm and in this way to break through the personal, the subjective, making the personal general, as indeed life always does. . . . "[13] The stories' given societal framework denies their characters a mature, fulfilled adult existence. Once they leave childhood behind, they must choose between two paths: either to adapt to the status quo or to evade social integration altogether. The path of conformity is ruinous. It leads to brutal white supremacy (Mr. Slatter, Mr. Macintosh), exploited femininity (Molly Slatter), prostitution ("A Road to the Big City"), and crime ("Hunger"). But neither can the individual be saved by resisting integration. This is demonstrated by "Leopard" George in the story of the same name, a settler who becomes a guilty party in the life-death cycle despite all his efforts to remain uninvolved, or by the "Non-Marrying Man," who drifts back and forth between stifling white society and the native bush. He is an African Wandering Jew who will never fit into either realm. And the children of the veld, as shown above, are granted only a temporary reprieve.

The logical conclusion of Lessing's African stories is that human beings, if they are to save their dignity and sense of justice, must escape from the "disgraceful scene" of a society whose very existence depends on violent segregation and exploitation of the weak. It was undoubtedly in this spirit that Lessing herself left Africa before her thirtieth birthday. The gradual sequestration of the individual from an oppressive society, arrived at only by implication in these stories, will be carried out step by step by a single figure, Martha Quest, in *Children of Violence*.

Children of Violence I-IV

Lessing began intensive work on the first volume of this cycle shortly before the publication of *The Grass is Singing* in 1950. The series was to include five novels and to occupy her intermittently for nearly twenty years. It consists of *Martha Quest* (1952), *A Proper*

Marriage (1954), *A Ripple From the Storm* (1958), *Landlocked* (1965), and *The Four-Gated City* (1969). As the fifth volume has but little in common with the preceding four, it will be discussed separately in chapter five.

The biography of Martha Quest shares with the first novel its basic theme—a young person exploring the avenues (primarily just dead ends) open to her in stifling South African society. But the treatment of the subject matter here is radically different. This is reflected even by the divergent style: the terse, intensely earnest and analytical diction of *The Grass is Singing* contrasts with an expansive, uneconomic, even plodding prose, which in turn mirrors the plot development. The heroine advances in intricate spiral circles, rather than in a straight line toward her doom. *Children of Violence* is set in an eclectic "composite of various white-dominated parts of Africa,"[14] which Lessing calls Zambesia. She emphasizes that this is a fictional country not intended to resemble the historical Zambia. Further, it is important to stress that, while Martha Quest's confrontation with South African society is undoubtedly inspired by Lessing's own experience, it would be shallow merely to label the books "autobiographical novels." Any one-to-one identification of heroine and author would be a misrepresentation of the novels' substance.

In the violent society of the African stories, the only being with a chance for survival is the child, whose ethical instinct is not corrupted. Accordingly, we meet precocious Martha Quest, whose unsubtle surname alludes to the search for meaning which is to follow, while she is still largely in childlike harmony with nature. She roams the veld of her parents' farm, defiantly toting Havelock Ellis's treatise on sexuality, warily conscious of the adult society she is about to enter. The reader accompanies her through various phases in her pursuit of intact vision and fulfillment. These may be roughly summarized as follows: integration into mindless social life and the dubious thrills of dating (vol. 1); marriage and motherhood (vol. 2); political activism and immersion in ideology (vol. 3); and finally, personal and political disillusionment and departure to another realm (vol. 4). While Martha's private entanglements always run parallel to her developing political consciousness, the former predominate in the first and second volumes, while the latter is of greater importance in the third and fourth. The series, which has been the subject of numerous scholarly studies,[15] was reprinted in 1970. *Martha Quest* and particularly *A Proper Marriage*—one of Lessing's most humorous and entertaining works—have won widespread acclaim with readers. *A Ripple From the Storm*, on the other hand, has been called "as stultifying as Martha Quest's own psychological paralysis,"[16] claustrophobic and boring. While definitely not Lessing's greatest achievements, these texts are significant as her first lengthy examination of the leveling of the individual by society's institutions.

   Children of Violence can again be interpreted as the verbose diagnosis of a "fragmented" personality. Martha perceives successive fragments of reality astutely, but cannot integrate them to form a whole. This is illustrated by the many passages describing her exhaustive self-scrutiny, during which she perceives her separate physical, emotional, and intellectual selves as severely disjointed. The novels are sustained by a repetitive pattern: the idealistic Martha runs headlong into a given collective identification, from which she promises herself "wholeness," fulfillment, and "freedom." Actual experience quickly disillusions her, and she fervently severs the bond in order to try another route. This episodic structure is something like a room of many doors: the reader observes the obstinate opening and closing of each one, but remains in the original chamber—Martha's mind. The structure conforms to that of the classical *Bildungsroman*, the "novel of development" which leads an impressionable protagonist through quintessential confrontations with societal and cultural institutions to finally build his or her character to full-fledged maturity. This very goal of harmonious plenitude, next to unobtainable in modern times, has rendered the genre largely a product of the eighteenth and nineteenth centuries. Lessing, however, employs it deliberately, its limitations notwithstanding. When she gives her heroine (by second marriage) the surname Hesse, she is clearly alluding to Hermann Hesse, author of one of the great German *Bildungsromane, The Glass Bead Game* (1943; Engl. trans. 1949). Her relatively unmodified use of this genre in a modern setting accounts to a large extent for the first four volumes' sluggish effect on many readers.

Martha strikes out into the world with the immediate need to escape her mother's influence and the long-range compulsion to avoid ever becoming like her. May Quest, a figure probably more memorable than the author intended, plays an important role in the first two volumes (she is awarded an apotheosis of sorts in the fifth volume, *The Four-Gated City*). She is a prototype for Lessing's conception of the female role within conventional, dead-end marriage: her life is an orgy of self-denial, her frustrations all channeled into self-pity, nagging, and "busybodying." May Quest incenses Martha through reactionary racial prejudice, (she hates blacks, Jews, and Greeks), her conformist mentality and Victorian sense of morals. In short, her very existence is an insult to all of Martha's ideals.

Martha seeks a counterconcept to Mrs. Quest, one which will save her from repeating her parents' mistakes. In principle, this should not be difficult, since Martha is well-read and immersed in social theory of

every kind. At fifteen, she is a self-proclaimed atheist
and socialist. She constructs a fantasy of a just society,
freed from oppressive racial and sexual codes: "There
arose, glimmering whitely over the harsh scrub and the
stunted trees, a noble city, set foursquare . . . its citizens
moved, grave and beautiful, black and white and
brown together, and these groups of elders paused . . .
and approved these many-fathered children" (I, 11).[17]
In practice, the search for an ideal society or even the
"real, ideal friend" turns out to be full of pitfalls. Her
rebellion against stifling role stereotypes inevitably
takes the shape of equally meaningless substitutes.
When she leaves home to work in the city, her needs are
extremely conventional: a major part of *Martha Quest*
describes her initiation into dating, buying clothes,
"sundowner parties," and the various time-killing rituals of the privileged white "Sports Club crowd." As a
rare white-female newcomer, prized in this male-
dominated, closed society, she is quickly assimilated in
a way which leaves her the individuality of a manne-
quin: she indeed does fulfill this function for her first
boyfriend, who is obsessed with dressing her smartly.

Lessing's interest in schizophrenia rises to the surface here. From the outset, Martha diagnoses her own
"divided self": one part of her, given the flippant nickname Matty, acts out banal roles, while Martha, the
intellectual "detached observer," looks on. Thus her
intellect quickly perceives that she is caught in a stereo-
type but, instead of extricating herself, she runs deeper
into variations of the same role.

Throughout the series, Martha tries to counteract
societal injustice through her personal liaisons. Acutely
aware of the stigmatization of Jews (a favorite object of
May Quest's invectives), she plunges first into a sexual
relationship with Adolph ("Dolly") King, a Jew bitterly
conscious of his pariah status. Martha is motivated by
the need to "show" the Sports Club crowd, as she

"showed" her mother, that she is not bound by their conventions. This need overrides her resentment at "having her first love affair with a man she was not the slightest in love with" (I,184). The affair is cut off by the intervention of the very crowd it was supposed to infuriate, and Martha is left deeply depressed.

Her slap in the face of convention having backfired, she tries a second avenue of self-realization when she marries Douglas Knowell. A conventional marriage is precisely what she had intended to avoid, but again her convictions and her actions are strikingly discordant: "she was revolted; she thought he looked vulgar and ugly . . . She said to herself that now she could free herself, she need not marry him; at the same time, she knew quite well she would marry him; she could not help it; she was being dragged towards it, whether she liked it or not" (I,243). At the end of the first volume, Martha's essential condition has not changed. She is still motivated by fear that circumstance will cheat her out of a full life. She is haunted by a sense of "terrible urgency" (I,246), and powerless against the magnetism of collective behavior.

Martha's marriage, described in *A Proper Marriage*, is as conventional and unfulfilling as her dating whirl. Following patriarchal protocol, she makes the mistake of defining herself by her relationship to a male, and assures herself about her husband, "He's a man, at least." But Douglas Knowell is not to be the "ideal friend" Martha seeks. His very speech mannerism of doubling words ("But that-that was rather-rather a strain") makes him symbolic for inevitable repetition: in this case, Martha's duplication of her mother's mistake in entering an unhappy marriage. The institution of marriage is equated in Lessing's work with bondage— we are reminded of Mary Turner's fateful union, or the short "Story of a Non-Marrying Man." By marrying, Martha temporarily sacrifices any hope of self-fulfillment, but she is as powerless as was Mary Turner to resist taking the step.

The main achievement of *A Proper Marriage* is its sardonic description of the effects of pregnancy and birth on the female consciousness. Though the rare British female novelist before Lessing dared to discuss female sexuality in print, it was not until the 1960s that the theme really began to shed its taboos.[18] In fact, Lessing is credited in the United States, where censorship laws were very conservative well into the second half of the twentieth century, with having considerably liberalized the tolerance of both readers and publishers.[19] Thus *A Proper Marriage* again places Lessing among the pioneers. Through Martha's (highly idealized) preoccupation with sex, Lessing illustrates that much of what happens to Martha is motivated by biological drives, which may run entirely contrary to rational decisions. Further, Lessing brings cogent arguments against the glorification of motherhood: "One saw a flattering image of a madonnalike woman with a helpless infant in her arms; nothing could be more attractive. What one did not see . . . was the middle-aged woman who had done nothing but produce two or three commonplace and tedious citizens in a world that was already too full of them" (II,274).

Martha's frequent perception of her body as a depersonalized object reflects society's assessment of her: for the doctor she is merely a healthy female body, for Douglas a sex object which can be tied down by motherhood, for the state she is the potential bearer of docile subjects. Lessing is among the first novelists to tackle the issue of state-controlled abortions (a question still hotly debated thirty years later), when Martha lashes out against "governments who presumed to tell women what they should do with their own bodies; it was the final insult to personal liberty" (II,92).

The implications of Martha's pregnancy are nevertheless ambivalent. Technically, it is merely a further knot in the ties of conventionality. On the other hand, the condition of pregnancy puts Martha temporarily back into touch with primeval nature. This is emphasized in a memorable scene in which Martha, and an equally pregnant friend, go swimming naked in a roadside bog during a thunderstorm. Martha is likened to a passing frog: she is at one with the water, in Lessing's work always a symbol of healing and harmony. Yet the natural fulfillment of pregnancy is quickly broken by the institutionalized humiliations of the delivery in a production-line maternity home, later by the realities of caring for the child, which Martha deeply resents.

In fact, the baby has simply replaced Douglas, who is away at war, and who infuriates Martha by his unexpected return. Though she now knows her marriage is doomed, "Matty" lets herself be railroaded into the purchase of a house in a "nice" neighborhood, further cementing her marriage, before she breaks away. The self-declared individualist Martha acts in accordance with traditional femininity, passively following the man she secretly considers a ninny and a boor.

Martha finally separates from Douglas, leaving her daughter Caroline to be raised by a stepmother. She is unmistakably glad to be relieved of the motherly role, which she found uncomfortable and false to begin with, and believes other women can fill better. Thus at the end of the second volume, she has eliminated both bourgeois marriage and motherhood as viable collective identifications. Though these two concerns have dominated her search for meaning, she has been constantly aware of the political and societal unrest surrounding her. She has always known that Douglas fully subscribes to the oppressive white-supremacist hierarchy, considering all political dissidents "cranks." He comes to embody for her the "self-displaying hysteria" of the local right-wing newspaper. Accordingly, her

rejection of conservative marriage goes hand in hand
with her leaning toward liberal political activities associated with the Communist party: "Though there isn't
one yet, but if there is I shall join it" (II,304). Again,
Martha attempts self-realization through "joining," be it
the Sports Club or the socialist underground. The lesson
she must learn is that all institutionalized groupings tend
to level and cripple individuality.

A *Ripple From the Storm* chronicles the activities
of Martha's socialist group, which divides and sub-
divides, and has its main function as a mooring post and
sounding board for the raising of Martha's consciousness. The political technicalities involved here are not
of great interest to the general reader.[20] Martha deliberately works herself into a state of nervous exhaustion—a
strategy employed by all Lessing heroines in search of
higher truths. But her susceptibility to repetition remains
unchanged: as in her affair with the Jew Adolph King,
she again tries to personify ideology by marrying Anton
Hesse, who is not only Jewish, but a German refugee,
model Communist, and "enemy alien." Like Douglas
Knowell, who first appears as a more or less likable
chum and sex partner but turns under Martha's scrutiny
into an hysterical, oversized baby, Anton Hesse also
undergoes a steady degeneration. At first glance a man
of steel, contemptuous of simpering personal problems
which only interfere with party work, he is soon
unmasked as a frightened and small-minded bluffer,
who clings to communist jargon as the last thread of
order in a chaotic world. His characterization reflects
Martha's successive disenchantment with both political
activity and marriage.

A *Ripple From the Storm* and *Landlocked* are
lengthy reckonings with the question of communism
and political activity. Martha sees communism not as a
sacred ideology per se—as Anton says, a Communist is
"a dead man on leave" (III,30)—but as the only alterna-

tive to a violent society in which five percent bore themselves swathed in pink taffeta at sundowner parties, while ninety-five percent die early of malnutrition, disease, and overwork. Through her initiation into communism, Martha learns to put her own importance in proper perspective. Her consciousness broadens from primarily egoistic perceptions toward an awareness of her surroundings. And from her work as a liaison between the black slums and the white do-gooders, it becomes clear to her that the violent gap between the two is too great for her to bridge alone.

Martha Quest comes to understand herself as the tarnished product of a deficient and violent social order: she reflects that she was born during World War I, and that her own child was born on the eve of World War II. The individual's development is determined largely by the armed conflicts which mark the century. This is the meaning of the title *Children of Violence*. At the end of the fourth volume, Martha has at least achieved the insight that neither conformity within a violent society (as a docile civil servant's wife), nor idealistic agitation against its ironclad institutions can bear fruit. The only solution is her departure from this framework, in hopes of starting a new life in England.

Before she leaves, however, she does find for a brief time the "ideal friend" she has sought, in the person of the Polish refugee Thomas Stern. Drastically more than Martha's, Thomas's life has been determined by violence. It is a miracle that he is alive at all, since all his family members were annihilated in concentration camps, which fate he narrowly escaped. Their relationship is doomed to be short, since Thomas, totally enmeshed in political strife, first travels to Israel, then goes into voluntary exile in an African village. Martha realizes anew the fragility, even with the help of "mystical" communication, of personal relationships between individuals marred by violence.

Three episodes at the end of *Landlocked* pluck up the series' thematic mainstays again: repetition, organized political action, and personal morality as a solution to societal evil. Martha's still chronic fear of repeating her mother's mistakes leads her to take final departure from her daughter Caroline. May Quest continually brings Martha and Caroline (who has been raised by Douglas's second wife) together, confronting Martha, as it were, with the living proof of her role-betrayal. But Martha ultimately refuses to admit to the child their true relationship, since the danger is too great that her daughter would come to hate her as Martha hates May. Thus, though increasingly wary of the pitfalls of repetition, Martha has made little progress in her methods of avoiding it. She still defines her female role negatively, that is, by not entering the mother-role embodied by May Quest.

The hopelessness of finding individual fulfillment in a violent world is expressed by the death of Thomas Stern, of which Martha learns shortly before her departure from Africa. The fever of which Thomas dies is apparently just as much existential as physical. His mental disintegration is recorded in chaotic memoirs, which Martha tries to edit. These notes have been interpreted as proof of "the unreality and lunacy of the kind of commitment [Martha] had while working for leftist causes."[21] This may describe one fragment of Martha's reaction. But far more important is the fact that these memoirs are the only personal document which accompanies her on her voyage into a new life. She cannot relinquish the idea that there might be sense and method in the apparent madness (the document will, in fact, play a central role in *The Four-Gated City*). Though Thomas's efforts to organize the fragments of his consciousness were futile, he does express the crucial idea that insanity is a rational answer to a violent society: "I tell you, Martha, if I see a sane person, then I know he's mad" (IV,116). The seed planted here will grow to maturity in the series' fifth volume.

Finally, the embers of Martha's belief in political organization are emphatically doused when she visits a meeting of younger left-wing activists. She and her one-time fellow agitators, now in their late twenties, are unabashedly referred to as has-beens and viewed with open mistrust. The uselessness of such meetings is established unambiguously afterwards as they realize "that while they had sat arguing in the stuffy bright little room, the skies had been swept by storms and by rain" (IV,280). In Lessing's juxtaposition of natural forces (the rainstorm) with human ideologies, the latter always appear feeble and artificial.

Children of Violence traces the footsteps of a single heroine through multifarious patterns of commitment in a highly ritualized society. Martha suspects that these collective rites are nearly empty of meaning—from the orgiastic celebration of her first wedding to the heated perorations of the arch-Communist Anton Hesse. Even her own political involvement appears ultimately as a counterritual. Thus the process of education underlying the *Bildungsroman* seems, at the end of four volumes, to have totally disoriented the heroine, rather than propelling her toward her right place in life. But she has to sample and experience the patterns of social conformity before she can transcend them. Lessing's statement regarding "the individual conscience in its relations with the collective"[22] is, therefore, that individuality cannot thrive in the ritualistic affiliation with society's institutions and counterinstitutions. Equally, the individual must laboriously tread the path *through*, and not *around* these collectives on the way toward wholeness of vision.

3

To Breed Something Better Than Ourselves: British Novels 1956-1962, Plays and Poems

Retreat to Innocence

Lessing's fourth novel, published in 1956, occupies a singular place in her work. Many of her readers are unaware of the book's existence—it is her only novel out of print, since she has refused to allow its reissue. Her opinion of the book is disarmingly objective: she not only recognizes its weaknesses but has repeatedly expressed her wish that it would disappear for good: "It was a wonderful theme, but I did not do it justice."[1]

Lessing conceived of and wrote the novel in 1954-1955. After her first literary successes with *The Grass is Singing* and *This Was the Old Chief's Country*, the need to secure her place in the literary forum with regular new releases was evident (while, as she correctly predicted, the Martha Quest cycle was to be a long-term undertaking). The literary climate was conservative, and the challenge to a young, liberal female author—competing with "old guard" writers such as Graham Greene, Somerset Maugham, and J. B. Priestley, as well as the "Angry Young Men" John Wain and Kingsley Amis—was considerable. Symptomatic of the prejudices of the day was the back cover of *Retreat to Innocence*: "Although very much an attractive young woman, Miss Lessing's social views and her provocative novels mark her as one of the first among a rising generation of brilliant young social critics."[2] The implicit contradiction between being a "brilliant social critic" *and* an "attractive young woman" is disturbingly clear. Thus, Lessing apparently set out to write a book not lacking in reader appeal, but nevertheless apt to make a clear-cut social statement on the issues of crucial concern to her at that time.

The book sets up, almost like a laboratory experiment, the fusion of the totally political being (Jan Brod) with the passionately nonpolitical being (Julia Barr). Jan is an exiled writer from Czechoslovakia, Julia the spoiled daughter of wealthy, liberal aristocrats. Their mutual attraction, undeniably, is mainly sexual. The focus of the experiment is on Julia, who is impervious to historical and political thought, which she describes as all "filth and dirt and heroics." Nevertheless, she pursues her first sexual involvement with Jan, closing her ears to his arguments, both private and political. She meddles, partially by means of her father's influence, in Jan's personal affairs, employment, his publication endeavors, and entanglement with the Emigration Office. Though she means well, she is totally incapable of dealing with the British bureaucracy (wittily characterized by the fictional figure "Miriam Hauptmann," used by civil servants to taint the files of unwanted immigrants). Julia succeeds only in upsetting the delicate equilibrium of Jan's life: he loses his job and is denied citizenship. He finally returns to Czechoslovakia, leaving her to marry the inane junior-executive Roger Metland.

Julia Barr is Lessing's first case study of the coming generation: the children of those "children of violence" who trained their social and political consciousness on the atrocities of two world wars and the emergence of communism. This second generation, whose liberal upbringing backfires completely, is to play a vital role in Lessing's works, particularly in the early 1960s. Julia is the perfect reactionary to everything represented by her parents: where they embraced sexual and religious freedom, progressive politics, and equal education for all, Julia's ideals can be summed up by a frothy white church wedding, Billy Graham revival meetings, and the resolute evasion of all thought-provoking ideas. As Jan Brod observes, "the great men of the nineteenth century said God was dead and that man could be God—but they didn't know that in 1955 'the younger generation' were going to resurrect God in the shape of a handsome young American from the Middle West with a nice little wife and some plump well-fed children, and all financed by American big business" (74f.).

In this vein, Julia clings to oversimplifications about life: she "loves" Jan but "hates" everything she doesn't understand because it gets her "mixed up" and threatens her "happiness." Motivated by fear of repeating her parents' lives, which she sees as emotionally barren and artificially complicated by political chit-chat, she adopts the fifties' handiest cliché as a model for her own life: "I want to get married young and have four children and no war, and to be happy. That's all" (67). To emphasize her lack of internal substance, Lessing characterizes her largely through her external surroundings: chameleonlike, she takes on the personalities of the rooms she enters. Her frilly, childish bedroom reflects both her refusal to grow up and her love of ornate bourgeois settings, and contrasts with Jan's simple room, which is dominated by a portrait of Gorki hanging over the bed. Her wavering between Roger and Jan is expressed through the alternative of student café or immigrants' hangout. When truly trying to sort out her muddled emotions, Julia is unable to enter any room, and spends a whole night wandering through London. The novel's conclusion leaves her in yet another room: the "warm dry cave" of a taxi, in which she takes refuge along with the massive purchases made for her imminent wedding. No matter that her "clean, well-lighted place" is an illusion, its confining comforts as temporary as the next traffic jam. She clings to it. After all, "What's the matter with comfort?" (333).

Not inconsistent with the general climate of the mid-1950s, Julia sees personal comfort and political awareness as mutually exclusive. She stubbornly evades the latter ("It's not my fault") and though of course she senses that Brod's insights will forever contaminate the harmonious scenario of her marriage to Roger, her faith in mindless conventionality holds her to the path she has chosen. Julia, like Martha Quest, wrestles with the problem of a "divided consciousness." But in fact her intelligence is not sufficient to sustain the division plausibly. As opposed to Martha, she does not *want* to know the dimensions of her second self. Lacking Martha's rebellious spirit, Julia is perfectly content to assume the first comfortable collective identity that comes along.

Jan Brod is the book's main strength and in fact one of the most interesting characters in Lessing's early work. His loquacious musings are essential for any study of the author's relationship to communism in the 1950s. Jan combines psychological insight, personal wisdom, and a realistic assessment of the political situation in East and West with an absolute faith in a socialist future. The novel on which he has worked for ten years is an allegory likening the birth of communism to the birth of Christianity—an idea first developed by the German-American communist Wilhelm Christian Weitling in *The Gospel of a Poor Sinner* (1845; orig. *Das Evangelium des armen Sünders*), which describes Jesus as the first communist revolutionary. Jan predicts temporary setbacks for socialist thought (as exemplified by Julia Barr's generation) but never loses faith in its ultimate victory. The persuasiveness of his allegory is put to the test when Julia types the manuscript for him: she

doesn't understand a word of it, indeed, she deliberately closes her mind to what she is typing. Her utter
imperviousness to analytical argument—even to Jan's
poignantly simple sketch of her hypothetical confrontation with the paradigmatic revolutionary peasant
(225ff.)—lends support to Jan's decision to return to
Prague. She is living proof of the displacement of his
political ideals in conservative Britain. Julia is not far
from the truth when she concludes that "people like me,
we're already dead as far as [Jan Brod] is concerned"
(333f.).

The altogether too diffuse threads of Jan Brod's
characterization have apparently overtaxed some of
the book's readers, who prefer the comfortable one-
dimensionality of Julia Barr. It is a misinterpretation to
assert that *Retreat to Innocence*'s "central episode [is]
the love story."[3] On the contrary, the book's central
thrust is its political statement, which, in retrospect, was
entirely accurate: it proves and simultaneously bemoans
the cyclical movement of socialist consciousness with
the generations; that is, the necessity of "retreat" as a
counterforce to progress. In the equation set up between
the two generations, the missing catalyst for Julia's
consciousness-raising is the element of human suffering, which she has never known and which, accordingly, is irrelevant to her. Her efforts to imagine the
atrocities of war result in the drab images found in an
old movie. Nevertheless, since "at least one corner of
Julia's indifference has been eroded,"[4] a possible con-
tinuation of the dynamic cycle is implied—perhaps to
be carried on by a mature Julia when the clichés of the
1950s have run their course.

The Golden Notebook

The chaos of modern ideology, politics, and sex

roles, to which Julia Barr had no answer other than mindless retreat, is again the central conflict in the much more complicated novel *The Golden Notebook.* Published in 1962 and read in many translations all over the world, it is still Lessing's most popular work. Many literary historians describe it unequivocally as her magnum opus. It is by a wide margin the subject of more critical studies than any of her other novels and is virtually a classic in every feminist's library. Despite its length (666 pages)[5] and complexity, *The Golden Notebook* makes a coherent single statement through its congruity of form and content: It defines "fragmented consciousness" as both the natural result of life in our torn century, and at the same time as the arch-enemy of a purposeful existence.

The novel focuses on a writer, Anna Wulf, living in London in 1957 from the modest royalties of a best-selling novel and unable to write another book. Its form is carefully, even mathematically constructed. A framework novel under the ironic title "Free Women" constitutes approximately one-fifth of the total text and is divided into five sections. These are interspersed with Anna's four notebooks, the total of which represent the remaining four-fifths of the book. Completing the symmetry of this scheme is the fifth, the golden notebook, which synthesizes the other four notebooks in a compressed description of the breakdown and reintegration of Anna's personality.

The formal arrangement of these narrative fragments reflects the novel's content: the dialectic opposition of chaos and order within the protagonist's consciousness. Early in the book, Anna asserts that the problem of chaos is at the heart of her artistic struggles. She is too realistic not to recognize the chaotic nature of twentieth-century existence, but nevertheless clings to the hope that on paper she can somehow make sense of things. While suffering from a compulsion to write, she sees that any effort to condense her generation's experience of wars, violence, and many-fronted revolutions into one book could only end as "a mess." By keeping four separate notebooks, internally divided by a system of lines, spaces, and newspaper clippings, Anna Wulf attempts to impose a rational (if artificial) order on the fragments of life as she perceives them. The implied abolition of a coherent, traditional fictional form corresponds exactly to the impossibility of a harmonious, streamlined *Weltanschauung* for the protagonist.

The notebooks are a chronicle of Anna's biography from 1950 to 1957, with lengthy flashbacks describing her experience in World War II in Africa. The superimposed novel "Free Women" takes place in 1957. We meet a politically disillusioned Anna, further wounded by the end of a recent love affair, who devotes a great deal of effort to her friend Molly and Molly's troubled son, Tommy. Anna's moral energy is gradually drained through Tommy's suicide attempt, exploitative boarders, and meaningless love affairs until she finally collapses. In the fifth section of "Free Women" she has recovered and is preparing to go into welfare work.

The notebooks' content can be roughly summarized as in Chart 1.

Chart 1: Summary of notebooks

BLACK:

A
f
r
i
c
a

Anna's experiences in Africa during the war; fruitless negotiations regarding TV and film rights to her African novel, *Frontiers of War*; reviews of this novel. Clippings relating to violence in Africa.

RED:

C
o
m
m
u
n
i
s
m

Anna joins the Communist party in 1950. Reflections on the development of the communist dream in the early 1950s and on Stalinist politics. Anna's hopes for a new, uncorrupted party in England are dashed; in 1956 "People are reeling off from the C.P. in dozens, broken-hearted" (448). Newspaper clippings on violence in general, and on current events such as the Rosenbergs and McCarthy.

YELLOW:

F
i
c
t
i
o
n

A novel on which Anna works intermittently, entitled "The Shadow of the Third." Fictionalization of Anna's relationship to Michael through the journalist Ella's prolonged love affair with Paul, a psychiatrist. Ella's disillusionment with communism coincides with the end of the affair. Ella approaches mental breakdown and concentrates her own writing efforts on the male/female conflict.

BLUE:

D
i
a
r
y

Anna enters psychotherapy because "she cannot deeply feel about anything. She is frozen" (234). Newspaper clippings on H-Bomb, Korean War. The year 1954 marks both the end of her affair with Michael and Anna's withdrawal from the Communist party. Her shaken mental balance is aggravated by affairs with Nelson and DeSilva. Affair with Saul Green leads to breakdown and recovery.

GOLD:

| S y n t h e s i s | Anna "cracks up": in her "mad" state, experiences, characters, and situations of the other notebooks flash before her eyes like a film. Final section of the golden notebook is a fictional piece written by Saul Green, Anna's partner in madness. |

Despite Anna's attempts to separate and classify the aspects of her experience, the borderlines between the notebooks are permeable. All phases of the notebooks are interconnected by clippings on current events, and by common themes such as violence, communism, and sexuality. In addition to their dynamic influence on one another, Anna's gridlike[6] rubrics of experience, once given the fourfold division, self-divide repeatedly, reminding the reader of spontaneous cell division. The breakdown and categorization of experience, once initiated, appear self-generating.

The initial catalyst for this process is unambiguously political. The dispersion of Anna's perceptions is closely related to the historical situation; specifically, to the drastic upheavals within the Communist party in 1956 when the Soviet Union made a show of brutal power by invading Hungary. Droves of disillusioned Communists, many of them intellectuals and idealists like Lessing, found their faith in organized communism permanently shaken and left the party. The shattered communist dream plays a crucial role throughout Anna's four notebooks and can safely be equated with the fragmentation of her entire viewpoint. Her whole sense of purpose in life crumbles with her admission that the "great dream has faded and the truth is something else—that we'll never be any use" (53). The breakdown of her political ideals is equivalent to the breakdown of her personality.

The single structuring force in this process is Anna Wulf's consciousness. Where the Julia Barrs of the world do not even perceive the rifts in modern society, the analytical Anna is not only painfully aware of the world's every injustice, but paralyzed by a feeling of personal guilt for *all* suffering, from the game pigeons in Africa to the victims of Auschwitz. She becomes obsessed by the shreds and fragments of a violent world. The unmistakable sign of her "cracking up" is her uncontrollable compulsion to collect newspaper clippings. Since she can no longer mentally organize their content, she clings to an illusion of order by pinning them by the hundreds on her walls. Anna is ultimately released from her compulsion by the realization that no single human consciousness can encompass the world's suffering and make harmony out of chaos. Her ambition to "make sense" of the twentieth century's atrocities has been an expression of cowardice, the lie of a crisp notebook cover over an incoherent scribble. But while the communist movement appears to be in for internal chaos and decades of setbacks, there is still hope on a personal level in the "small endurance that is bigger than anything."[7] Her new respect for the "small endurance," illustrated by the metaphor of the Sisyphus-like boulder-pushers, frees her to write again, despite her certainty that the product will contain no universal truths. Ironically, she then writes the traditional short novel "Free Women," employing the same artificial, objective fictional structure which the notebooks have denounced.

The real victims of the constellation drawn by "Free Women" are of course the *un*free women and children—Molly's son, Tommy, and his stepmother,

Marion. Tommy, like Julia Barr of *Retreat to Innocence*, stands for the younger generation who have
grown up amidst their parents' political and ideological
agitation. He sees his mother, who acts minor roles and
dabbles in left-wing politics, as a mess and a "failure."
On the other hand, he despises his big-shot father,
Richard, a tycoon, whose thrills in life are gained by
making money and chasing skirts. Anna correctly diagnoses that children like Tommy suffer from too many
choices, resulting in "paralysis of the will." Instead of
clear rights and wrongs, his parents have given him
moral arguments he is unable to assimilate. Anna's
dream that Tommy is her own infant, starving for lack
of milk from her withered breast, is an expression of the
older generation's failure to provide inner nourishment
for their children. Tommy's suicide attempt directly
follows his reading of Anna's notebooks and his realization that she, despite her years of experience, can no
more make sense of things than he.

For the younger generation, personal deficiencies
become the mainstay of self-definition. When Tommy
manages to blind, if not kill, himself, he becomes a
"whole person" at last, as Anna ironically observes. The
"terrible damage" to which she refers is not his loss of
vision, rather the stunting of his psyche. But its physical
counterpart in the form of blindness forces everyone to
acknowledge his handicap and frees him from the pressure of behaving in a normal way and succeeding in life.
This makes him happy for the first time.

Not surprisingly, Tommy allies himself with a fellow victim of the given constellation, Marion, his
father's alcoholic second wife. The case for feminist
consciousness is made primarily through Marion, and
not through Anna and Molly. Marion lacks their intelligence, self-irony, and analytical capacities. She has
clung to Richard with the tenacity of a desperate
animal, and his loss of interest in her means the destruction of her self-respect. Tommy's suicide attempt cor-

responds to the low point in Marion's morale; almost constantly inebriated, she wallows in misery because her husband no longer loves her. Only through Tommy, who sees his father realistically, does Marion gradually experience the feminist "revelation": she has sacrificed her self-esteem to a common bully. Concurrently, with Tommy's prodding, she begins to take an interest in world affairs, since her marriage no longer functions as the center of the universe. Though Marion's political enlightenment has more to do with flat sentimentality than with conviction, she nevertheless manages to free herself from her degrading dependency on Richard. Marion's exemplary situation—blind adherence to an exploitative marriage at the cost of her self-respect—formulates in a nutshell the feminine fallacy of the 1950s, which was soon to come under fire from the women's movement, incipient at the time of *The Golden Notebook*'s publication.

Thus the book was originally read by many as a feminist treatise, contrary to Lessing's conviction that *if* the world survives the cataclysms of this century at all, "the aims of Women's Liberation will look very small and quaint."[8] Undeniably, the novel's major conflict is between the individual and historical progression, and not between males and females. Nevertheless, a feminist reading is reinforced by Lessing's deliberate emphasis on the role of sexuality in Anna's reflections. Like certain heroines of D. H. Lawrence, Radclyffe Hall, and others before them, Molly proposes that she and Anna are a "completely new type of woman" (4). Anna refers repeatedly to the sex war, parodies the tears cried "on behalf of womankind," and plays the role of "the white female bosom shot full of cruel male arrows" (636). The fictional figure Paul asserts at one point that "the real revolution is, women against men" (213). It is therefore justified to ask exactly how feminist Anna Wulf's reflections are.

The "free" women see the very evasion of tradi-

tional sex roles as a victory in the sexual revolution.
Molly's self-respect derives from the fact that she has
not taken shelter in marriage. Unfortunately, marriage
is replaced by damaging love affairs. Anna enters casual sexual relationships on principle, trying to shed the
"feminine" motivation (love) in favor of the "masculine" ones: curiosity, mere physical attraction, friendship, opportune circumstances. Despite her determined
sexual experimentation (which typically leaves her
depressed), it is evident that Anna's real desire is identical to Marion's: she wants to be loved in a conventional
relationship and fears that she never will be. Anna
rejects some modalities of male-female relationships,
but by no means does she make a breakthrough toward
feminist self-awareness. She remains male-oriented,
and resents even the physical condition of femaleness,
as demonstrated in a much-quoted scene during which
her day is ruined by the onset of her detested menstrual
period. Neither physically nor spiritually has she seen
herself as complete since, as she confesses to Molly
early in the book, having been "ditched" by Michael.
She maintains a flat with extra space held ready for a
man and repeatedly laments the fact that "real" men
have been replaced by homosexuals and overgrown
babies. Anna (like all Lessing's protagonists) is repulsed
by nonheterosexual relationships. This is demonstrated
by her conflict with the homosexual boarders, Ivor and
Ronnie, who represent violent and malignant hatred of
females, against which she is powerless: "she, the independent woman, was independent and immune to the
ugliness of perverse sex, violent sex, just so long as she
was loved by a man" (407). Clearly she is anything but
"free" from sex-role stereotypes; in fact she is dangerously close to describing her own condition when she
speaks of her psychoanalyst as "traditional, rooted,
conservative, in spite of [her] scandalous familiarity
with everything amoral" (5).

Anna's male-fixation is further demonstrated by the treatise on female orgasm (214ff.). While this is not the place to expound on the long tradition of theories on this subject, in general Anna's viewpoint coincides with the school established by Sigmund Freud maintaining the superiority of vaginal over clitoral orgasm: "There is only one real female orgasm and . . . everything else is a substitute and a fake" (216). This idea was emphatically disputed by Masters and Johnson's *Human Sexual Response* (1966), but since then a major branch of sex research has returned to Freud's (and Anna's) premise.[9] In any case, it is definitely a male-oriented theory, considered by many to be a direct descendent of Victorian concepts of sexuality. Anna's view of female orgasm reflects her belief that she cannot attain personal fulfillment in the absence of a male partner, however disappointing he may turn out to be.

Accordingly, the final episode in her cracking up requires a male catalyst, Saul Green (and his counterpart in "Free Women," Milt), whom she prescribes "for herself like a medicine" (648). She grins but does not really balk at the stereotyped half-hope, "Perhaps this is *the* man" (654). Saul Green is in fact a *deus ex machina* of sorts—here, as in other Lessing texts, the American Male symbolizes the future, for better or for worse. The reader encounters a similar type in Cy Maitland, a "healthy savage" and brain surgeon, who gloats over all the lobotomies he has performed and supports McCarthy because "well, he's right, we can't have the Reds taking over" (327). Saul Green, on the other hand, is a writer in self-exile from McCarthy's America. He is both physically and emotionally ill, avoids all personal responsibility, and is a compulsive liar. His rampant egomania is matched only by his sexist attitudes: as a "full-blooded American boy," he sees his female partner as "a broad, a lay, a baby, a doll, a bird" (559).

Nevertheless, Anna falls in love with Saul, only to

see her own fragmented personality reflected in him.
He is a multiple schizophrenic, who unpredictably
assumes and sheds half a dozen personalities. At the
same time, he rattles out the word "I I I I I I I I I I" like
machine-gun fire. He has no conception of time or even
of his own age. Anna and Saul slowly absorb each
other's personalities—they give the dissolution of their
respective fragmented consciousness full rein and sink
into madness for a week. Anna relinquishes, finally, her
tenacious intellectual command on life. In a process
exactly converse to that undergone by Marion, who had
to discover that there *is* a world beyond her personal
misery, Anna has temporarily to abandon her compulsive awareness of the outside world in order to regain a
sense of self. She has been crippled by her social conscience: "I was desperately ashamed, being locked in
Anna's, an unimportant little animal's, terrors" (588). In
madness, Anna finds the isolation and introspection
necessary for the reintegration of her personality.

For whereas Saul prefers to remain "crazy in a
good cause," Anna (whom the reader perceives as
essentially sane all along) will return to lucidity for the
sake of Janet, her adolescent daughter who is due home
from boarding school. If Saul and Milt have no reason
to care about the next generation, Anna does: Janet is
"why I'm sane and you're nuts" (661). In contrast to
Tommy, the perpetual reminder of his parents' failure,
Janet represents the positive function of the up-and-
coming generation. For the sake of her normality
(achieved, ironically, at the expense of her individuality), Anna will pull herself together and go on as before.

Nevertheless, the saving insight is that in madness
there is hope. Looking back on *The Grass is Singing*, we
recall that madness in the form of Mary Turner's disintegration, lost sense of time, and apathetic introversion,
appears there as the last stage of psychic ruin just
preceding physical death. *The Golden Notebook* marks

a revised, much more subtle station in Lessing's evaluation of madness. The word runs like a leitmotif through the book, as Anna repeatedly tries to define what it means to "crack up" and where the process begins. Like Martha Quest, Anna diagnoses her own schizophrenic tendencies—many experiences "split" her, leaving one part of her to act out a role, the second "curious detached sardonic" alter ego to observe and stave off her own collapse. Both she and Molly have been through psychotherapy with a therapist they name "Mother Sugar." This name implies two things about becoming well-adjusted through therapy. First, that it depends on role stereotypes reminiscent of the Eternal Womanly-Motherly; second, that adjustment is a self-deceptive sugarcoating over reality. Anna crumbles this sugarcoating of apparent sanity in her week of madness, dispensing with the omniscient guardian of sense and causality. She takes on personalities of various people whom she has known, while Saul assumes the form of an untamable and destructive tiger. Anna is now freed from her compulsion to see the world as sensible, orderly, and progressive. Instead, her eyes are opened to "the dark secret of our time": that despair and madness are everywhere, normal reactions to an insane world. Madness is a "cocoon," a place of self-nurturing and growth.[10] This insight frees Anna to set off into the world once more, secondarily as a writer (we know that she writes "Free Women"), but primarily as a marriage counselor and social worker for delinquent children.

The release of Anna's writer's block marks the resolution of another major conflict—fiction versus reality, more specifically the function and responsibility of art with regard to society. This conflict builds on a long literary tradition which reached one zenith with the contentious theories of realism, symbolism, and naturalism in the nineteenth century. Of more direct relevance to Lessing were the doctrines of socialist realism, developed by the Communist party in the 1930s. These guidelines required that literature depict reality in a historical setting that illuminates its relationship to class struggle and, if possible, that fiction achieve a didactic effect by increasing the reader's understanding of socialism. Among other critics of this aesthetic conception, Albert Camus pointed out in 1957—the year in which *The Golden Notebook* takes place—that socialist realism can have little to do with "reality" as long as the real world is not predominantly socialist. Lessing, as a member of the Communist party and participant in an authors' delegation to Moscow in 1952, scrutinized the viability of these doctrines for her own writing. Though she has always seen the written-to-specification products of socialist realism as "intolerably dull and false,"[11] her literary figures reflect her involvement with socialist thought in that they are analytically aware of their place in the greater historical and political framework. Anna's artistic block expresses her numbing, nagging fear of leaving the doctrines of communism completely behind her. She cannot write about her subjective dilemmas, for fear she will obscure the much greater miseries suffered for the sake of the revolution. Her writing is hindered, as she puts it, by Chinese peasants, Algerians, Cuban guerrillas—all those who are still fighting for the social revolution in which she has lost faith.

This conflict between art and truth is introduced in the novel's first scene, when Anna ponders the idea that our chaotic world makes art "irrelevant." She doggedly assures Mother Sugar, in a scene described later, that she can no longer really believe in art. On Tommy's questioning, she admits, "I keep trying to write the truth and realising it's not true" (274). Both she and Saul wrestle with the fact that in describing things—their duty and compulsion as writers—they "button up" and tidily dismiss their substance. Nevertheless, Anna plays the game of "naming," in which she tries to envision her real place in the universe by naming every piece of it (548). At the same time, she often denounces the nomenclature she chooses as "all lies." Anna's ambivalence toward art results in a split of her perceptions into four fictional levels. Given the personage Anna as a point of reference for "reality" (and discounting for the moment that she is of course Lessing's fictional creation), she tries to get at the truth of her own experience through diaries and journals (level one). Within these, she sketches short stories and the novel "The Shadow of the Third" (level two). Her protagonist in this novel, in turn, attempts a further fictional distillation of truth by writing a novel about suicide (level three). And finally, the dialectic relationship between the notebooks and reality is encompassed by the superimposed narrative frame in the form of "Free Women." This is a fictional approximation of the idea incorporated in the portrait of a painter painting a painter painting a painter. As Anna realizes toward the end of the book, the divisions in narrative distance have taken her progressively *further* from the truth, not closer to it. The medium dominates the substance: even the healing madness of the golden notebook is expressed through the medium of cinema, and not as unmediated reality.

Despite Anna's conviction that words are incapable of expressing truth, the conflict is ultimately won by her even deeper belief in the writer's moral obligation to enlighten—better imperfectly than not at all. "We spend our lives fighting to get people very slightly less stupid than we are to accept truths that the great men have always known . . . violence breeds violence. And we know it. But do the great masses of the world know it? No. It is our job to tell them" (618).[12] *The Golden Notebook* is thus, among many other things, a large-scale presentation of the artist's paradoxical position— her "small personal voice" may not contain existential truth, but it nevertheless speaks up in behalf of the "people who are inarticulate, to whom one belongs, to whom one is responsible."[13]

A by-product of this conflict is the novel's evaluation of traditional literary forms. It has been described as Lessing's farewell to realism. By dividing the "objective" fictional product ("Free Women") from the quantum of muddled experience contained in the notebooks, the novel calls attention to the enormous gap between the quixotic human condition and its literary manifestation in the realist tradition. The reader cannot help but perceive the smooth traditional novel as limited, in contrast to the masses of material preceding its formulation. Though it is persuasive enough in context, the logic of this equation depends on an artificial either/or construction (i.e., superrealist fiction or none at all, absolutely intact consciousness or mental breakdown) which ignores the long tradition of innovations on the often multilayered fictional consciousness since Joyce. Certainly Lessing's verdict that realism (which in 1957 she called "the highest form of prose writing") gives but a fragmented picture of "real" consciousness is anything but new to literature, but it is a major step in her own artistic progression. Paradoxically, *The Golden Notebook*, while stating the impossibility of formal harmony in the novel, is Lessing's masterpiece in the art of narrative construction. In it she attains complete command over the techniques of novel form, which were not fully mastered in its predecessors.

Anna Wulf's multifaceted microcosm is a reflection of the world situation in the late 1950s, when the end of the Stalin era marked a drastic reorientation of the political Left, when atomic catastrophe seemed imminent, when individuals saw themselves more and more threatened by giant political machinery and ruthless capital. Individual attempts at creating "order" of such a world lead to fruitless compartmentalizing and ultimately to the erosion of mental balance. This is Lessing's most forceful attack on boxed, parceled, and labeled thinking. Anna Wulf abandons with a sigh her four notebooks, through which she had hoped to make sense of the world's chaos. She chooses, instead, the small, individual endurance. Her repudiation of labeled collectives is a major step on the way toward a glimpse at the true whole of human experience, which will advance into the center of Lessing's focus in her post-*Golden Notebook* novels.

Plays and Poems

Though Lessing is best known for her novels and chooses that genre for most of her production, she has also written plays and poems intermittently throughout her career. Many of her novels contain sequences of poetry, and *Fourteen Poems* was published independently in 1959. She has written five stage plays:

> *Before the Deluge*, produced London 1953 (also produced 1958 under the title *Mr. Dolinger*);
> *Each His Own Wilderness*, produced London 1958;
> *The Truth About Billy Newton*, produced Salisbury, Wiltshire 1960;
> *Play With a Tiger*, produced London 1962 and New York 1964;
> *The Singing Door*, published 1973.[14]

In addition, she has written four scripts for television plays: *The Grass is Singing* (1962), *Please Do Not Disturb* (1966), *Care and Protection* (1966), and *Between Men* (1967). Her literal translation of *The Storm*, a play by Alexander Ostrovsky (1823-1886), was produced in London in 1966.

Of Lessing's plays, only *Each His Own Wilderness*

and *Play With a Tiger* have received wide acclaim. Her main interest in the theater spans the years from 1958 to 1962, and was no doubt inspired by her work as a substitute theater critic for *The Observer* for a few weeks in 1958, during which time she wrote five critiques.[15] The plays of this period were written concurrently with *The Golden Notebook* and are thematically related to it. As that novel is the result of Lessing's deliberations regarding the viability of the novel form (and her own virtuosity in handling it), it is not surprising that she explored other genres at the same time.

During Anna's mad scene in the golden notebook, she remarks, "I must write a play about Anna and Saul and the tiger." She alludes to *Play With a Tiger*, written in 1961. Its protagonists are Anna Freeman and Dave Miller, an American. Both are socialists, idealists, rootless on principle, and in search of something better than humanity's status quo. The play opens with traditional setting and dialogue, but moves progressively away from external reality (by removing props) into the psychological realms inhabited by Dave and Anna. Lessing deliberately uses a naturalistic opening so that the audience is not only unprepared but "pleasantly shocked"[16] when the walls of reality are literally dismantled at the first act's conclusion. In an orthodox application of Freudian dream analysis, Dave and Anna slip into a sequence of roles through which they act out their own psychic development—Anna rejects her parents' conventional marriage, Dave rebels against the shallow American middle class. Tormented by the idea that the human race is doomed if it fails "to breed something better than we are," Anna suddenly has the vision of a tiger. It first purrs docilely, then lashes out and covers her with wounds. Associated with the uncageable Dave, the tiger symbolizes the awesome strength and irrational destructiveness of human nature, on which the future depends.

The play relies not only on the friction between realist and psychological drama, but also on tension in language and diction. The constant juxtaposition of Dave's cliché-laden, modish American jargon and Anna's monosyllabic, at times searchingly earnest and always educated remarks lends the play its particular stylistic and intellectual appeal. Language signifies character here—Dave, whose antibourgeois status is in fact only a detour around responsibility, ultimately chooses the path of least resistance by marrying Janet Stevens, who expects a child. Anna rejects the temptations of conventionality, breaks an engagement she sees as individuality-threatening, and is left at loose ends and unsure of the future—but true to her ideals.

Play With a Tiger, like *The Golden Notebook*, has been interpreted as a feminist work and produced, to Lessing's chagrin, as a "self-righteous aria for the female voice."[17] Its major accomplishment, however, lies not in any ideological thrust but in its technique. By removing the backdrops, it destroys the stage-made illusion of reality and replaces it with the characters' subconscious. Whereas psychological delvings are easily attainable in a novel, they are much harder to sustain in a drama, which depends on action and dialogue. Thus Lessing subtly modifies the medium to suit her needs, taking as the play's mainstay not the solution of a *dramatic* conflict (the subplots involving Janet Stevens and other minor characters are rather banal appendages), but the exploration of the protagonists' mental and emotional depths.

The struggle between the generations, carried out by Anna, Molly, and Tommy in *The Golden Notebook*, provides the central conflict for *Each His Own Wilderness*. The play was premiered on 23 March 1958. On the whole less subtle than *Play With a Tiger*, it again focuses on a middle-aged socialist, Myra Bolton, at a crossroads between past and future. She tries to alleviate her sense of fragmentation by means of journalistic and political activity and through her relationship to her son. The younger generation, however, reject all "causes" and vacillate between the neurotic need to drop out and the equally neurotic compulsion to conform. They scorn their parents' supposedly liberated mores and seek merely the security of an eight-to-five job: "What's wrong with being ordinary—and safe? . . . We are bored with all the noble gestures. . . . Leave us alone to live. Just leave us alone. . . ."[18] The play ends with Myra's insight that her intellectual, liberal stance has failed on two counts. It has not assuaged her sense of personal isolation, and it has backfired with the second generation, who appear as self-indulgent cowards on whom their parents' agonizing is largely wasted. Lessing's treatment of the younger generation, a common theme in British drama of the late 1950s, would suggest comparison with the dramas of John Osborne and other contemporaries. In striking contrast to Osborne, however, she embellishes her depiction of the generation conflict with a good dose of humor and thus establishes an ironical distance between the action on stage and the spectator.

But Lessing does not take the next logical step and make use of the stage as a didactic tool to examine the forces responsible for the protagonists' isolation. As opposed to her novels, which always mobilize social criticism, the plays restrict their argumentation in large part to the individual case study. The influence of Bertolt Brecht, felt in England, for example, in Osborne's *The Entertainer* (1957) or in the works of Arnold Wesker, is absent from Lessing's dramas. In a 1972 postscript to *Play With a Tiger*, she denounces dramatic realism as the "greatest enemy of the theatre." Clearly Brecht's development of the epic theater as a catalyst for real social change made little impression on Lessing. Thus her plays remain more or less unexceptional in the context of British theater of their time. They share with many other dramas the theme of the isolated individual, who delves into the past and the psyche in the course of the play, only to stand relatively unaltered at its inconclusive closing. Lessing's characters are further typical for the late 1950s' extreme disenchantment with ideologies, movements, and great ideas. Caught between the ideological ballast of the past and the prospect of a mindless, middle-class future, they are effectively paralyzed, prisoners of their own disillusioning insights.

If Lessing's plays are little known, her poems, written sporadically throughout her career ever since the early 1940s, are virtually obscure. They have been tactfully ignored by critics. *Fourteen Poems* was published in an exclusive edition (five hundred copies) in 1959, and a few poems are scattered in newspapers and journals.[19] Three poems appear in *Going Home*, and poetry fragments serve a minor function in the opening scenes of *Retreat to Innocence*. More recently, the delirious hero of *Briefing For a Descent Into Hell* includes lyric passages in his ravings, and *Marriages*, the second volume of Lessing's newest series, makes extensive use of poetry and song sequences.

In the poems of the late 1950s, as in the narrative works, an undercurrent is supplied by the dialectic juxtaposition of civilization and nature. Lessing frequently uses imagery in contrasting pairs (sea/land, darkness/light, silence/sound). The "Dark Girl's Song," for instance, contrasts the colorful resilience of nature (the sea) to the pallid coldness of human constructions (canals, spires). Nature appears as *the* single source for the rebirth of humanity in form of the "New Man," a theme borrowed from literary expressionism of the early twentieth century:

He comes
    He comes

> From the salt sea
> From the salt land
> Sky-high figure up the breaking sands
> Puddles sky-white around his climbing feet
> Breakers thundering behind his fists.
> Sea drums
>   Earth drums
>   Sky drums
>   [...][20]

Like "New Man," nearly every early poem by Lessing
utilizes the recurring image of water. Its presence
means salvation and hope; its lack signifies dulling of
the spirit and even death. The water image is crucial in a
comparison of the two versions of "In Time of Dry-
ness," published both in *Going Home* (1957) and *Fourteen Poems*. Where the earlier version's last stanza refers to water twice (waterfalls, bright drops), it has
been stricken from the later version, which thus—its
imagery relying totally on aspects of drought—is by far
the more cohesive and ultimately more forceful poem.

Lessing's early poetry shows a strong affinity to
that of older poets such as T. S. Eliot or even James
Joyce, rather than to contemporaries. She adheres
(though not without visible effort) to traditional rhyme
and meter schemes. Almost all poems are written in
iambic (and occasionally trochaic) meter, and recourse
to forced rhyme is not infrequent (grieve/live). Within
these traditional formal boundaries, however, the diction is elliptical and abstract, the individual stanza
condensed to its essentials of image and atmosphere.
An unusual element is added by dialogue verses which
imply a splitting of the lyrical "I." It is the friction
between tradition and experimentation which gives
these poems their intriguing, if not earthshaking, quality.

An afterthought to this kind of poetry appears in
Briefing when the protagonist Charles Watkins lapses

occasionally into verse. Though his poesy impresses the
reader at first glance as anachronistic, this assessment is
complicated by two facts: first, that the "poet" is in a
state of delirium and heavily drugged; second, that he is
by profession a classical philologist to whom verse
forms are of course second nature. Poetry takes on
more significance in this novel when it is used to under-
line the refrainlike aspects of the litany with which we
socialize children:

> Be a *good* baby, I'll rock you to sleep,
> He is a *good* baby, he has always slept a lot,
> He is a *good* baby, he doesn't give any trouble,
> He is a *good* baby, and he has always slept the night
>   right through.[21]

The use of poetic refrain in *Briefing* to demonstrate
a social function rather than a literary statement paves
the way for Lessing's poems a decade later. In the novel
Marriages Between Zones Three, Four, and Five, she
stresses the process of poetic oral tradition, rather than
the individual poem, as a means of communication.
One of the book's central leitmotifs is the songs
recorded by the Zones' historians or chroniclers. These
songs are used in medieval minstrel fashion, as simple
ballads which explain the ways of the "Providers" to the
citizens and inform them of the doings of the royal
court ("Cold and dark your wedding bed/O King, your
willing bride is dead"). In addition, the singing of songs
indicates to the chroniclers the direction and extent of
migrations across the Zones. Particularly the women
and children of Zone Four communicate in verse,
which they use to keep their race's most important
traditions alive. When Al·Ith, the new queen, uncon-
sciously absorbs their lyrics, it is a sign of her true
assimilation into the Zone. The narrator notes that when
a song emerges from her subconscious, she suddenly

finds meaning in it which would not be heard by the casual listener.[22] Thus poetry appears here not only as an historical record but as a universal medium. While the verses are routinely learned and sung by all citizens, they contain hidden significance which is gradually revealed to certain individuals at crucial stages in their lives.

In this respect, Lessing's latest use of verse builds on a long literary tradition, starting with the Greek chorus, whose function it was to interpret the protagonists' actions. More relevant in our century are the songs of the Brechtian drama, used, precisely as are the songs of Lessing's chroniclers, to awaken consciousness after they have been absorbed and chanted by rote. Thus, as interesting as the poems themselves is the author's varying employment of poetic forms at various stages of her career. After 1960 she abandoned, with few exceptions, the traditional imagery-laden love poems. Her renewed interest in verse some two decades later then restricts itself to the subgenre of the ballad: the only poetic form which conveys a miniature epic development. Lessing's weaving of songs and ballads into the narrative fabric bespeaks both her basic disregard for traditional genre distinctions and, at the same time, her essential loyalty to prose.

4

Habits and Temptations:
British Stories

Lessing's first fictional portrayals of the British milieu took the form of short stories. Many of these were written concurrently with the African stories, starting in the early 1950s. The established system for classifying Lessing's short prose works is unique in that it relies on the simple aspect of geographical setting rather than the usual criteria of style, theme, or chronology. This fact alone attests to the inseparability of Lessing's fiction from its specific historical/national context, and indeed, an unmistakably British flavor permeates the stories set in Albion from the very beginning.[1] These stories demonstrate Lessing's narrative prowess at its finest. Unfortunately, the unjust modalities of literary criticism often have it that even a mediocre novel will command more attention than the most sensational short story. Lessing herself comments that the market for stories is less than encouraging.[2] Recent criticism suggests that a fair appreciation of these works requires their upwards revaluation in toto, as a unit "greater than just the sum of the individual stories."[3] Despite these snags in marketing and reception, Lessing's short stories are, to state it simply, extraordinarily good reading and would, even if she were known for them alone, guarantee her reputation as a virtuoso of realistic prose.

The focal point of nearly all the British stories is a modern European individual. These protagonists are steeped in civilization and culture, thus in radically different circumstances from their solitary African counterparts, but they share with them the fight against existential, if not demographic, isolation. The stories' structure is dialectic: each protagonist comes into conflict with a given collective force, and wrests from the ensuing battle her or his identity and self-definition. The collective forces involved generally fall into five categories: sexuality, role crisis, politics, history, and social ills. Through her concentration on the exceptional and crucial individual experience, Lessing abides by the traditions of the short-story genre. Yet the individual appears not as an isolated quantity, but rather in silhouette against a larger collective backdrop. Through this double focus on the human consciousness *and* the forces that move it, Lessing broadens and enriches the genre in a characteristic way.

Of the thirty-five British stories, a good half have sexuality as a central motif. Examination of their own sexual roles is the single avenue traveled most frequently by these stories' personae in their search for self. We recall *The Golden Notebook*'s thumbnail sketches for short stories (in the final pages of the yellow notebook), nearly all united by the upbeat "A man and a woman . . . ." In the British stories, this theme comes to full fruition. The relationships shown here range from the quotidian to the bizarre and taboo; sexual encounters can express anything from neurotic spite to supreme bliss. The latter extreme is poignantly expressed in "Each Other." The story describes a brother and his newly married sister who are obsessively enamored of one another. During their clandestine early-morning meetings, they play a ritualistic game with the ebb and flow of sexual climax. For Fred and Freda, "normal" sexual mores are inverted. Their bastion of incestuous ecstasy is the only pure good in a threatening and immoral world. Freda's marriage was intended to lend a cover of respectability but, instead, it cheapens and taints their intimacy. They are on the "edge of disaster"—both little more than adolescents, he threatened by unemployment and she by a distrustful husband. Near-metaphysical sexual communion appears here as the only refuge from hostile reality.

In other stories, sexuality is exposed as a weapon used to denigrate females. Lessing frequently adopts a male viewpoint to demonstrate this mechanism. This technique is flawlessly convincing, as in general the male and female viewpoints are represented with equal insight and auctorial sympathy. "Mrs. Fortescue" describes an adolescent boy who suddenly realizes that the grandmotherly tenant of the apartment overhead, whom he has known all his life, is in fact an aging prostitute. He gradually works himself into an anguished fever of repulsion and desire, until one evening he enters Mrs. Fortescue's flat and rapes her (with her more or less indifferent sanction). The sexual assault is followed by a verbal one ("Filthy old whore, disgusting, that's what you are, disgusting!" [II,144]).[4] Fred's own sexual initiation, obviously a by-product of his irrational revenge on Mrs. Fortescue for being an "old tart," leaves him with a sense of triumphant superiority over women in general. More important than the story's exceptionally convincing portrayal of the adolescent's sexual ambivalence is the fact that Fred appears *not* as an exploiting brute, but as a victim of his own misunderstood drives and, in a broader sense, of a sexually repressive society.

The theme of sexuality as a statement of male domination is developed most incisively in "One Off the Short List." Lessing has described this as one of her favorite stories.[5] Graham Spence, a middle-aged, might-have-been writer distinguished only by mediocrity, compensates for his dashed ambitions by systematically compiling a list of women he considers worthy of

his seduction. He then savors the brief illusion of con-
quest, which dulls the taste of his general impotence.
Lessing's psychological penetration of the Don Juan
syndrome is superb. Spence, a failure and flunky in all
respects, sees himself in the role of the victor when
playing the ladies' man. He is thus a living illustration of
Simone de Beauvoir's observation that even the puniest
male becomes a "demigod" in his own eyes when he
compares himself to a female.[6] His illusion is shattered,
however, by his encounter with Barbara Coles, whose
refusal to be flattered by her inclusion on Spence's "list"
only aggravates his determination to ravish her. She
puts him in the position of "raping a woman who was
making it elaborately clear he bored her," but instead of
relenting, he grows even more hostile. He feels "dis-
like," "anger," "annoyance," "jealousy," and finally
"hatred." The latter word is used no less than nine times
during the seduction scene. Spence's self-respect rests
exclusively on the fact of his maleness, which enables
him to "have" women—sex, for him, is an antagonistic
function of a crippled ego. Coles, on the other hand,
personifies the total separation of sexuality from intelligent and substantial communication. She cannot be
reached, much less "conquered" by the pest who
refuses to leave her apartment. Despite all his ob-
sequious, manipulative, exploitative behavior, Spence
is also a pitiable victim of a competitive and sexist
society, whose "losers" take refuge in sexual games
which only further degrade them. The story turns over
the stone of machismo to reveal a writhing worm of a
man who has no other place to hide.

    Though not always accompanied by the sheer sex-
ual desperation of "One Off the Short List," the network of roles and obligations governing male-female
relationships is an ever-present motif in the British stories. It provides the starting point of "To Room Nineteen," one of Lessing's most moving and multidimen-

sional texts. The story traces the fate of a woman who does everything "intelligently," from her well-matched and timely marriage, to the wisely spaced children, to the sensibly mortgaged house in the suburbs. As required by the patriarchal rule by which she abides, Susan gives up her own apartment to marry, and then her profession to raise her children. In her midforties, she stands at the center of a complicated configuration of household and parental duties, community ties, possessions, payments, and social engagements. The paradoxical result of her endeavors is a well-oiled middle-class machine in which Susan's presence is altogether superfluous: "all this depended on her, and yet she could not understand why, or even what it was she contributed to it" (I,355). As she oversees life being lived by others, she is increasingly aware that she has no life of her own. She becomes depressive, alienated, and finally begins to lose her mental balance. She imagines her house to be haunted by devils (the story is, incidentally, a house-fetishist's delight), and embarks on a search for total solitude, which she finds in a seedy hotel room. Here she sits and stares into empty space, drugged by the opiate solitude, which she is determined to preserve despite her husband's efforts to track her down. Not only expendable to, but increasingly threatened by, her own Frankenstein's monster—the bourgeois suburban paradise in which her husband has a mistress, the house a maid, and the children a competent *au pair* girl—she finally turns on the gas in room 19 and drifts "off into the dark river" (I,378).

Susan Rawlings's paradoxical fate—she is ruined by the very achievement of her goals—is more than a "failure in intelligence" (I,343).[7] It is symptomatic of a greater paradox, namely that it is in fact irreparably wrong to do everything "right" by society's standards. Susan's mistake was to sacrifice her selfhood to the bourgeois status quo, symbolized by a house which is not a refuge but a cage. The story clearly implies that without the colossal middle-class apparatus to tie her down, and without a patriarchal system to require that she cheerfully welcome her bondage, her personality would never have been eroded to the point of breakdown and suicide. "To Room Nineteen" examines the condition of the "well-adjusted," socially successful individual *in extremis*. Her comfortable niche is a cell padded by role expectations, possessions, marital games, and mortgage payments: all of which finally become her nemesis. The role crises which inevitably jostle such constructions provide the basis for many of the British stories (e.g., "A Man and Two Women," "Not a Very Nice Story"), in which the results are less drastic. But in "To Room Nineteen," the deadening effects of conformity are presented with sufficient voltage to force the reader's gaze beyond the protagonist herself, and onto an oppressive society, which, given the right circumstances, easily manages to push essentially sane people over the edge.

Gender-specific roles such as Susan's are a function of the greater societal framework always visible in these stories. Whereas her reaction to it is personal and introspective, other protagonists are shown in their roles as cogs in the big political wheel (Jack Orkney), as witnesses of specific historical situations ("The Day Stalin Died," "The Eye of God in Paradise"), or as outcasts who may quietly slip through society's loosely woven "safety net." "The Temptation of Jack Orkney" relates a situation comparable to "To Room Nineteen." This story focuses on the midlife crisis of a man who sees he has become expendable to the object of his previous fervent devotion, in this case not a bourgeois marriage but a political machine. As Susan Rawlings resignedly commits suicide, "because she had not got the energy to stay" alive, Jack Orkney leaves England for Nigeria because "he had not known what else it was he could do" (II,316). Both characters reach the analogous insight that their importance as individuals has been played out, whereas the greater machinery will roll on. Both are unable to reconnect with their once-meaningful collective affiliations.

"The Eye of God in Paradise" depicts, similarly, two tolerant British citizens grappling desperately for a rational focus on a given historical situation. They visit Germany in 1951, determined to suppress their memories of German atrocities and aggressions during the war years. While at this time (two years after the founding of the Federal Republic of Germany) the whole of the German population was anything but prosperous, the British situation was equally critical: hunger, housing shortages, food rationing, and difficult working conditions were the order of the day. The contrast between the British and the Germans is magnified here by the specific setting, "O ——," presumably Oberstdorf, a haven for Americans and wealthy tourists. Thus Mary and Hamish, fatigued British doctors, are confronted (in a skillful anticipation of the coming economic miracle) with robust and affluent vacationers. They cannot help feeling bitterness at history's contradictions: "Six years ago these people were living amid ruins, in cellars, behind any scrap of masonry that remained standing. They were half-starved, and their clothes were rags. An entire generation of young men were dead. Six years. A remarkable nation, surely" (I,167).

Mary and Hamish's general apprehension is brought to a first climax by a Dr. Schröder, who pursues them in hope of attaining connections which will help him get to the United States. He is one of Lessing's most impressive and malevolent characters, a mixture of the diabolical and the pathetic, and a symbol of postwar Germany itself. His facial skin, burned off in combat, has been carefully mended by grafts: "the whole highly-coloured,

shiny, patchy surface, while an extraordinarily skilful
reconstruction of a face, was nothing but a mask . . . "
(I,173). The deformation extends, of course, to his
menacing personality. A patchwork surface of conge-
nial hospitality just barely covers his underlying manipu-
lation and coercion of others. Despite the political
reformation of Germany, Schröder's pre-1945 convictions remain. He admits to having been infatuated with
"our Führer," who may have overdone things a bit but
nevertheless had the country's best interests at heart.
Schröder thus represents to the tolerant British a land
split by a schizoid division of appearance and historical
reality. A shining mask has been tacked over a wretch
who, by all rights, should bear the scars of guilt and
defeat. Instead, he not only appears healthier than the
shabby conquerors, but stubbornly clings to the convictions that have wrought so much destruction. The story
repeatedly contrasts surface order with internal decay
to back up this point.

A second meeting after the British couple's departure from O—— only confirms their unease. They visit a
distinguished colleague, Dr. Kroll, an aristocrat, artist,
and the esteemed director of a mental hospital. Here he
has himself locked up six months of every year. He is,
no less than Schröder, a schizophrenic. This is expressed
by his paintings, half of which portray unmatched natural beauty, while the other half are macabre and gruesome, with surfaces "like the oozing, shredding substance of decomposing flesh" (I,209). Their conversation
with Kroll makes it clear that he aided the Nazi program
of "social hygiene," i.e., sterilization and/or extermination of the mentally ill. His Third Reich notions remain
unchanged: he still straitjackets children and believes a
"quick and painless death" is often the best solution to
mental illness. At Mary and Hamish's disgusted departure, he gives them a photograph of his masterpiece oil
painting: a picture of lush paradise, in the center of

which glares an evil black eye, "the eye of a wrathful and punishing God" (I,218). The picture is a symbol not only of Schröder and Kroll, but of the schizophrenic historical role of Germany itself: for centuries the wellspring of music, art, and philosophy on one hand; between 1933 and 1945, the source of history's most unthinkable atrocities on the other.

The story makes a clear statement on the relationship between the individual and history. Lessing's emissaries across historical borders represent the optimum of enlightened, rational philanthropy. Nevertheless, no amount of individual tolerance can compensate for the magnitude of the recent historical past, and Mary and Hamish are sucked into a quicksand of fear and distrust. The initial physical restoration of Germany has little to do with healing, but is rather a grotesque mask over the past's ugly truth—a truth that will lose its menace only when real changes in consciousness occur. Where Mary and Hamish are perhaps too much aware of the past (both having lost loved ones in the war), Kroll and Schröder are only too ready to reassemble the pieces and go on as before, each safeguarding his personal advantage by whatever means necessary.

"An Old Woman and Her Cat" is not based on a specific historical setting but presents social criticism applicable to all modern industrialized countries. (In this respect, it is comparable to "England versus England," which diagnoses the painful position of anyone caught in a class-structured society.) The text employs a tried-and-true Lessing approach in that housing conditions symbolize the degree of an individual's integration within society and, in the case of the half-Gypsy Hetty, the extent of slippage downwards on the pole of respectability. Hetty is dependent for housing on the relegations of the housing council, and the reader witnesses her descent from a respectable single-family dwelling to tenement accommodations for the elderly.

Faced finally with the prospect of being sent to a rest home, where "the old were treated like naughty and dim-witted children until they had the good fortune to die" (I,166)—a place from which, adding insult to injury, her feline companion Tibbs would be banned— she chooses to disappear among the homeless on London's streets. She hides in a condemned house and peers down from a second-floor cranny as the frozen corpses of transients like herself are removed each morning by men who, while the "real citizens are asleep . . . make the rounds of all the empty, rotting houses they know about, to collect the dead, and to warn the living that they ought not to be there at all, inviting them to one of the official Homes or lodgings for the homeless" (II,172).

Hetty lives for a time from the pigeons brought by Tibbs, and eventually dies of cold and malnutrition. And Tibbs's fate applies in the greater sense to all of society's poor and aged misfits: though he "wished to be liked by the human race, he was really too old, and smelly and battered" (II,176) to find a new friend. He is rounded up with the other strays and "put to sleep." "An Old Woman and Her Cat" is a glimpse at a whole social framework—not an appeal for a single reform such as more low-cost housing (in fact it is Hetty herself who finally decides to avoid such housing). The story, told with empathy but decidedly without sentimentality, illustrates how easily society's anonymous members can slip down into the regions which are "no longer decent." It appeals to the reader's compassion for the maverick who cannot—or will not—be integrated in the "real citizens' " society. In this respect, the text is typical for all of Lessing's British stories. Their goal is illustration rather than agitation. Only in very rare cases do they leave the terra firma of realizm,[8] and tranquil meditations on nature are not infrequent ("A Year in Regent's Park," "Lions, Leaves, Roses . . ."). The individuals profiled here wander through the labyrinthine corridorš of sex roles, history, and politics, but most do not propound revolution or drastic change of any kind. What these stories do undeniably propagate is that the individual must be seen as both the product and the determiner of an intricate network of personal and extrapersonal factors. Lessing's singular examination of this network gives us not only characters whose habits, loves, failures, and successes are eminently readable, but also "the understanding that one's unique and incredible experience is what everyone shares."[9]

DORIS LESSING

Chart 2: MAJOR CHARACTERS OF
THE FOUR-GATED CITY

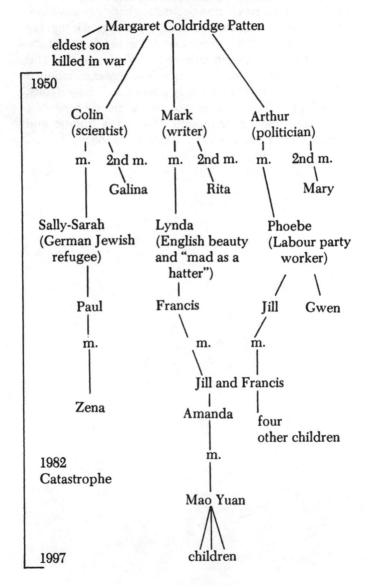

5

Toward the Evolution of Consciousness: *The Four-Gated City* 1969

If we wanted to single out *one* work which comes closest to spanning the entire spectrum of Doris Lessing's oeuvre—its substantial conflicts, motifs, images, and narrative techniques—it would be *The Four-Gated City*. This fifth volume of *Children of Violence* was published in 1969, exactly twenty years after the author's arrival in England, and concludes at long last the biography of Martha Quest. Martha, hotheaded individualist who took the bull of collectivistic society by the horns at a tender age, will also be the first of Lessing's characters to attempt an extrasensory, holistic vision of human consciousness. The experience of this single literary figure thus incorporates all three formative ideas of the entire works—individuality, collectivism, and the "whole." While *The Four-Gated City* stands in a direct line of descent from the early episode in which the fledgling Martha beheld a "noble city, set foursquare,"[1] shimmering on the African horizon, the novel also anticipates the new dimensions of Lessing's fiction in the 1970s and 1980s. It is both a second zenith (following *The Golden Notebook*) and a turning point within Lessing's production. Coming as it does from a renegade arch-realist, its conclusion may well be regarded as an intrepid and not unconvincing first attempt at future fiction. Seen in the context of the larger literary scene, *The Four-Gated City* is an exceptionally thought-provoking examination of society during and after the cold war—one of the sixties' best.

While this complicated novel unleashes in its 654 pages a bounteous potpourri of action, characters, plots, subplots and socio-historical background, the basic narrative process is still linear and traditional. The text is, like *The Golden Notebook*, artfully constructed. It is divided into four parts of approximately equal length, each consisting of four chapters, in apparent deference to the title. In analogy to the golden notebook of the earlier novel, *The Four-Gated City* culminates in a "mad" scene. An appendix then gathers in the many nets cast out by the foregoing chapters and binds them into a relatively tidy final knot. The novel relates the history of four Coldridge generations, from the matriarch Margaret Coldridge (by third marriage) Patten, to her grandchildren's children. A fifth generation (Amanda's children) is mentioned near the end. As the book progresses, fictional time is compressed into ever fewer pages. The narrative begins in 1950 and concludes around 1968; the appendix then takes the reader from 1968 to 1997 in some sixty pages.

The first four volumes of Martha Quest's biography have been described previously as a lengthy dialectic clarification of the individual's relationship to various collectives, in the *Bildungsroman* tradition. The final verdict reached there was that no collective identity—neither conformist sex roles, political affiliations, nor class status—is conducive to the search for real individuality. When we meet Martha again in volume five, she has left all these alliances behind and is miraculously cleansed of her urgent need to join and belong. In England at the age of thirty, she has shed her roles as May Quest's recalcitrant daughter, as Caroline's guilt-ridden mother, as Douglas's bubbly young wife and as Anton's comrade in revolution. (Only the union with Thomas Stern still lurks in her memory—the single relationship not imposed on her by societal or group pressures.) Martha enters her new life a *tabula rasa*, her confining affiliations obliterated. And she intends to keep things that way by making role abstention the major premise for building her second life.

This decision is one well worn by the heroes of the century's *Bildungsromane*. One might name only those of Thomas Mann's *The Magic Mountain*, and Hermann Hesse's *Demian*, *Siddhartha*, or *Steppenwolf*—all cast off the ballast of socially endorsed roles. By observing society from a distance, they strive for a higher form of consciousness and an absolute perception of the macrocosm. In this tradition, Lessing's heroine is best compared with Ulrich of Robert Musil's *The Man Without Qualities*.[2] Ulrich, unable to find his personal truth in the collective behavior patterns offered by the dying Austro-Hungarian empire, rejects all socially sanctioned "qualities" or roles—including any attempts at self-definition. Like Martha, he abandons his search for a professional or political calling in life around his thirtieth birthday. He then pursues a life without definable qualities, through which he hopes to enter the "other realm" of consciousness—a finespun state of intellectual/sensual perception. Even had Lessing not used a passage from Musil's novel as one of *The Four-Gated City*'s mottoes (156),[3] the parallel between Ulrich and Martha is clear—both live by the strategic refusal to let preprogrammed roles interfere with their personal growth.

Though Martha arrives in England penniless, she turns down two job offers, bound respectively to the political and the legal establishment. Both, she presumes, would tie her to a function defined and "named" by others. Instead, she fabricates names and backgrounds for herself in her chance encounters on the London streets. Her only uncounterfeited relationship is with Jack (further discussed below), who stands for pure sexuality—he is so possessed by the physical that abstract roles are of no consequence. Ultimately, Martha accepts a position as helpmate to the writer Mark Coldridge. Though the Coldridges are to be the mainstay of her adult life, her very commitment to them is possible only because her role in their house eludes conventional definition. She can function as the guardian of a monstrous family because the monster is not of her own making. The family members wrestle with the problem of naming Martha's role, which has endless variations—secretary, research assistant, housekeeper, friend, governess, and crisis manager. To the children—Mark's son Francis, his orphaned nephew Paul, and two nieces, Jill and Gwen—she plays a motherly role with humorous self-irony, heartened by the fact that she is not their biological mother (her daughter is in Africa). Her unconventional relationship with Mark and his mentally ill wife Lynda is a truly symbiotic triad, completely devoid of jealousy or possessiveness. On the contrary, Martha is a buffer zone between the estranged couple, and their *ménage à trois* frees all three from the roles they would be forced to adopt in a twosome.

Martha's refusal to be named and defined extends into the political realm as well. The Coldridge house is a hub of political conflicts, involving Communist party workers in all stages of commitment and disillusionment, stolid Labour party representatives (Arthur and Phoebe), the "Tory hostess" Margaret, and Mark's rebel brother Colin, who defects to the USSR. Mark is decried by the establishment as a Communist and by the Left as a capitalist. Even totally apolitical persons, such as Francis's friend Nicky Anderson, are sucked into political agitation through circumstance. Amid all this, Martha, whose previous political endeavors are known to the reader, listens and arbitrates. She attends the Aldermaston protest marches as one would a giant circus, but remains personally unmoved; organized political action can no longer tempt her. The mature Martha Quest is a figure whose aspiration to truer intellectual/ sensual perceptivity deprives her of the privilege of vehement emotions and conviction.

This "woman without qualities" withholds her acknowledgement of the given social framework because she is certain there is more to "reality" than the harried consumers of the 1960s realize. All the novel's characters, who struggle to adapt to life s rapidly changing façade, bear the battle scars in the form of personality rifts. They are either missing a dimension or, as often, live in bondage to one single dimension at the expense of all others. The latter are emblematic of a single-minded, fragmented approach to life: Phoebe represents blind support of the Labour party, Margaret equally blind backing of the governmental powers that be, Patty Samuels static adherence to the Communist party line. Colin lives only through scientific interest at the cost of personal responsibility, and Jill is character- ized by compulsive pregnancy. These figures are illus- trations of what *The Golden Notebook* diagnosed as compartmentalized thinking, that is, the neurotic drive to rely on *one* quality and concomitant inability to perceive the interworkings of the whole.

The characters with missing dimensions are more difficult to assess. Most extreme of these is Jimmy Wood, a "mad scientist" who does not appear mad at all, but is simply lacking a human conscience. This outwardly innocuous, humdrum fellow is perfecting his great invention, a lobotomization machine which will painlessly dissolve or alter the brain cells of problem- atic individuals. Dozens of governmental agencies are clamoring for the final product and are already using the experimental models. Jimmy Wood represents the alienation of science from the interests of humanity—a process all the more horrifying because its perpetrators do not even consider their nifty inventions unethical.

Also missing a dimension, particularly during his

teen-age years, is Paul Coldridge, son of Colin and
Sally-Sarah (whose very name expresses the division of
her person through exile—she commits suicide early in
the book). Paul's shortcoming is that "a moral sense had
been left out of [his] make-up" (357). His inability to
distinguish right from wrong manifests itself in adolescent kleptomania, a trait he sublimates through a
golden touch for business deals as an adult. It is important, however, that Paul is ultimately portrayed as a
kind and compassionate, if deeply disturbed, person.
He well illustrates that a defective moral sense in society's terms affects his status as a law-abiding citizen, but
not as a human being. This in effective contrast to
Jimmy Wood, who is an obedient citizen but an ethical
freak.

Mark Coldridge (and later his son Francis, to a
lesser extent) is also incomplete. He is "whole" only
when gallantly supporting the weak and dependent. As
Martha puts it, a section of Mark has been "put into
cold-storage" with Lynda, who finds his protectiveness
stifling. Lynda herself is the most important of the
damaged personalities, a schizophrenic blend of raving
beauty and "bedraggled slut" who has spent most of her
life in mental hospitals. Ironically, it is she alone—the
sole major figure in the book who is clinically
psychotic—who can finally point Martha in the direction of "whole" consciousness, as will be shown.

All these major and minor characters, with their
chronic crises and breakdowns, are scrutinized by Martha. She becomes "a person who watched other people
in a turmoil of living" (199). The only event that really
endangers Martha's equilibrium is her own mother's
visit. It forces her back into the dreaded role of dutiful
daughter, from which nothing short of May Quest's
death can release her. May, now old, embittered, and
unwanted, is the subject of a long and compassionate
portrait. Though loneliness has weakened her prejudi-

ces to the point that she even revises her hatred of blacks, she will never overcome her neurotic resentment of Martha, who epitomizes in her eyes a wicked world she can no longer understand. May is obsessed with her daughter's faults, real or imaginary. The proximity of mother and daughter drives them both into a state of desperation, culminating in May's near-existential release when, sent to the family psychiatrist, she is finally able to speak her mind, "and out of her flooded years and years and years of resentment, all focussed on Martha" (286). Thoroughly purged, May returns to Africa, where she dies a year later. The book brings the distressing theme of motherhood, which runs true throughout all volumes of *Children of Violence*, to a doleful close. May is tormented in her old age by her hatred of Martha. Martha, on the other hand, now a middle-aged woman, retreats at the prospect of facing her mother to a fetal position in bed for weeks at a time, unable to face life at all.

If the mother-daughter conflict is resolved with a vengeance in this novel, the motivic tension between civilization and nature, as built up in the earlier volumes, is further developed and refined. The book's two central images are "the city" and "the tree," particularly a sycamore which stands outside Martha's window.[4] Martha frequently gazes beyond the house in Radlett Street to see a tree sprouting or shedding leaves, according to its natural cycle, oblivious to the pollution (real and metaphoric) engulfing it. The image of the tree will reappear, with the same connotations, in the later novel *Shikasta*. Where the tree stands for nature's inviolable laws and rhythms, the city stands for culture and civilization. Martha's utopian vision of a good and just city motivated her to seek a new life in London, and it continues to tempt her there: "Somewhere in our minds there is an idea of a city. A City, rather!" (302). In England, however, she observes not the marvels but the

horrors of urbanization in a teeming and polluted megalopolis. Later, when her brainstorming with Mark
produces his utopian novel *A City in the Desert*, readers
assume it to be truth, and demand to learn its location so
they can emigrate. This reaction underlines the fact that
Martha is not alone in her dissatisfaction with contemporary city dwelling. Indeed, Mark does finally find his
life's mission in the founding of a City, actually a refuge
in Africa, which harbors fleeing hordes of British
citizens—and is financed, ironically, by American
capital.

Many of the book's lesser images and similes
reflect Lessing's unfaltering belief in the healing property of nature. Moreover, they attest to the essential
proximity of homo sapiens to the lower animals. One of
the most moving illustrations of this idea is Martha's
comparison of Paul, a desperate adolescent, to a caged
baboon she observes in the zoo, sawing at its bars with a
round pebble. "What fantasies or plans of revenge, or
hate, or escape did that poor baboon harbour, as it sat
there, with its round pebble, its only weapon, only
possession, pushed behind some straw?" (316). Society's teenagers share with its zoo exhibits their caged
status and the desperate, instinctive will to fight with
whatever means available—no matter how inadequate
the weapon and how hopeless the fight. The permeable
and elusive boundaries between all species are to be a
major motif in Lessing's later works, especially in her
next novel, *Briefing For a Descent Into Hell*.

But, humanity's primeval tie to the simpler beasts
notwithstanding, the modern citizens Martha observes
are caught in the deadlock of nature and civilization.
She sees them as somnambulant specters in the twilight
between the two realms, and repeatedly laments their
degeneration and denaturation into a race of "half,
uncompleted creatures. There they were, all soft like
pale slugs . . . their nervous systems were numbed by

the drugs they took to alleviate the damage done by the din they had chosen to live in, the fear and anxiety and tension of their lives. . . . They lived in an air which was like a thick soup of petrol and fumes and stink" (506f.). In this passage, Lessing speculates for the first time how this race would be viewed by extraterrestrial observers dropping in from space. They would find none of the gardens and fountains which symbolize humanity's harmony with nature—this harmony has been sacrificed to the wonders of civilization, that is, pollution, disease, and overcrowding. The individual's place in the environment is guaranteed only by a vicious circle of acquiring, possessing, and consuming. The players Martha oversees are tormented, their vision stunted by "a net of wants and needs that made it impossible for them to think of anything else" (507).

As she makes this observation, Martha is in a clairvoyant, rarefied state which enables her to actually visualize her place in nature. It is in such a condition that we first meet her in *The Four-Gated City*, when lack of sleep and food have supersensitized her perceptions, including her self-sure and hungry sensuality. For this reason she returns repeatedly to the libido-virtuoso Jack, whose brush with death in the war has left him permanently preoccupied with sex. Sexual acts are, for Jack, the only true proof that he is alive—a condition which, naturally, he wants to test as frequently as possible. Jack's life's work consists in assembling a harem of "my girls," who vary sexually from the near frigid to the nymphomaniac. He prides himself on assuaging all their anxieties. His house is maintained purely for the purpose of atmospheric and unusual erotic encounters. Though portrayed initially as a positive force, whose total sexuality complements Martha's exceptional connection with nature, Jack's development later in the book is revealing. Martha discovers that what once appeared to be a complicated ceremony in homage to pure sexuality has, in fact, evolved into a calculated system designed to "break in" girls for prostitution. Far from an elemental sensual force, Jack has become a cunning pimp, who accomplishes his goal with refined psychological warfare. Jack, too, has failed by committing himself to a single aspect—his compartmentalized obsession with sex has made him the personification of its perverse form, the violent and ugly sex described in *The Golden Notebook*. Even "natural," roleless forces must be held in perspective by an ethical rein.

Soon after Martha takes up residence in the Coldridge household, she becomes so absorbed by her duties that she "forgets" the heightened perceptivity of her first weeks in England. She will not regain it until many years later. The *forgetting* and *remembering* (or *knowing*) of higher truths is a central motif here and in later works. These watchwords stand for the ebb and flow of all human consciousness. This is Lessing's version of Plato's anamnesis theory—that all knowledge is really only recollection, a premise also crucial to the psychoanalytic methods developed by C. G. Jung. "Forgetting," that is, allowing oneself to become dull and unperceptive, is naturally the stronger of the two forces: thus Martha's next fifteen years pass routinely. She devotes herself to managing the heterogeneous Coldridge household and to her three-way symbiosis with Lynda and Mark. Many complications arise from the friction between the house's upper levels (in which dwell Mark, Martha, and the children) and its basement, frequented by Lynda, her roommates, and a string of clairvoyants, soothsayers, and soulsearchers. Lynda first occupies the basement with a matronly friend, Dorothy, also mentally ill. Dorothy is desperately trying to prove her recovery by becoming normal and competent. She demonstrates her stability by crocheting tea cozies, mothering Lynda, and dealing with everyday necessities such as plumbers and electricians.

Dorothy's downfall is inevitable, since she measures her competence against a standard which no longer exists—an efficient outside world. When Dorothy is discharged from the mental hospital, the industrialized Western world is already in that phase in which "nothing works." Her trials, as banal as the attempt to get new telephone books, take on nightmarish and truly Kafkaesque proportions. She not only fails to recognize the classical runaround for what it is, but even elevates it to a touchstone for testing her very sanity—and reaches the inevitable conclusion that she is mad and unfit for normal life, since she fails at the simplest tasks. Some months after her departure from the Coldridge house, Dorothy commits suicide.

Lynda Coldridge is the most multivalent and intriguing single figure in Lessing's work. Her reincarnation is implied at *The Four-Gated City*'s conclusion, and she reappears in the *Canopus* series. Like many mentally ill people during the 1950s, she has been subjected to shock and drug therapy to the brink of her tolerance. Her life in Mark's basement is a symbol of her having sunk beneath the surface of contented wifery into realms unimaginable for the sane and well-adjusted in the rooms above. Though she wants to get well, she equates sanity with the enfeebling and abhorrent rituals of a proper marriage, and chooses to remain mad rather than resume this role. When she finally repudiates her status as Mark's wife, her battle for sanity comes to hinge on her battle against addiction. Lynda's determination wins out, despite many setbacks, when she sees herself needed by Francis and Jill. The only force stronger than Lynda's illness and drug dependency is the necessity of guarding the future by nurturing the younger generation—a motif that remains unchanged in Lessing's work.

Martha, too, devotes many years to the volatile children, who often take precedence over her own concerns and over the occupants of the nether realms. But in her spare time she "works" with Lynda in long therapy or consciousness-raising sessions, which soon lead her to the conviction that Lynda's madness has its own validity.[5] When Martha is forced to nurse Lynda through a prolonged deranged phase, the book's (and Martha's) turning point is reached. She observes an emaciated Lynda, pacing the flat like an animal in a glass cage, as if searching for a way out (ignoring, of course, the doors and windows). This is a literal metaphor for Lynda's testing of life's boundaries. She has never definitively located the borderlines between "sane" people's reality and her own perceptions. Confined with Lynda in the basement, Martha (who has been intercepting other people's thoughts for some time) now begins to "remember." She learns to plug in to Lynda's wavelength of sounds, voices, and visions. Martha and Lynda agonize for a month, and Martha determines to continue at a later date her experiment with discovering what Lynda "knows."

She subsequently isolates herself in now-grown Paul's house, and continues her search, using nothing less or more than the classical mystic procedure—like Hesse's Siddhartha—of refusing sleep and nourishment. Martha's experiment with the metaphysical convinces her that the universe is filled with forces, or wavelengths, which affect everyone's subconscious, but which certain fine-tuned or supersensitized people (like Lynda) can intercept like a radio frequency. Whereas mystics traditionally seek to experience a form of god when tuned in thus, Martha encounters a devilish force she calls the "hater," which is responsible for much of humanity's atrocious and self-destructive behavior. Since ordinary people do not perceive the deafening sounds on the hatred wavelength, those who do are generally deemed "mad" when they describe the voices and visions they cannot switch off. This is not

Lynda Coldridge's singular fate, of course, but that of a prototype which goes back to antiquity: the mad (or blind) seer, who alone speaks the truth but is scorned by the world as a lunatic. Martha concludes that if our society could recognize and respect the extrasensory, Lynda would never have been declared ill. Martha's evaluation of Lynda reflects a second major step in Lessing's assessment of madness. The mentally ill are not sickly refugees from a sane world. Rather, their exceptional communicative and creative powers are a ray of hope in a system bogged down by mediocrity and conformism. This verdict is supported when, after the holocaust, Lynda and Martha use their telepathic powers to help organize the few survivors. *The Four-Gated City* suggests that truth has been suppressed by a jaded society for so long that it is only "through madness and its variants" (375) that certain truths can be found. Martha's personal view is: "Better mad, if the price for not being mad is to be a lump of lethargy that will use any kind of stratagem so as to remain a lump, remain nonperceptive and heavy" (510).

It is in this novel, and not in its more vehemently criticized successors, that Lessing's crucial change of focus is incipient. The book presents modern life's miseries as more or less given, and society's self-destruction as a foregone conclusion. Martha herself has given up trying to effect change, and swims resignedly with the stream of events. Her watered-down critique of capitalism reflects no more the fiery involvement, which she has seen to be fruitless, of her Zambesian days. The disillusionment of liberals like Martha is more than plausible—but is it enough to propose instead that one has merely to rouse dormant extrasensory powers in order to rise above it all? The logic behind the idea that going mad in a mad society will lead one closer to sanity is not exactly compelling. Many readers consider Lessing's implication "that radical change to save the human community from exterminating itself is accomplished not in direct political action but in madness and mutation"[6] a cop-out. For it ignores the magnitude of the world's *real* problems and dwells instead on visions of sugarplums—our potentially lovelier and finer perceptions.

Where Martha's mad scene transcends the limits of "realistic" consciousness and sensibility, the book's appendix discards once and for all the tenets of realism, formal harmony, and temporal continuity. Lessing has expressed her reservations about its success, saying that by the time she wrote it "I'd put myself into a damned cage . . . "[7] Nevertheless, the final pages of *The Four-Gated City* are among the best Lessing has written. Their "prophetic" theses seem less farfetched at this writing than they did perhaps fifteen years ago. They offer a cogent description of the increasing domination of individuals by technology and government after 1960, and a hypothetical sketch of the years from 1970 until the end of the century. The events are described in epistolary form, first by a long letter written in the late 1990s by Francis Coldridge to his stepdaughter Amanda. He tries to give her a picture of the years preceding the catastrophe, which took place around 1982.[8] He describes how he, Jill, and others built up a sprawling commune in the English countryside, until he replaced his father in Nairobi as director of the refugee city. His depiction of late-capitalist British civilization foreshadows the later novel *Memoirs of a Survivor*; it shows how humanity of Europe's last days, increasingly poisoned by radiation and pollution, gradually came unhinged. Individuals were just numbers in a giant data bank, crimes against property carried higher penalties than violations of human rights. Gangs ruled the streets and most people were neither fed nor housed, while a class of administrative royalty danced on the volcano, living in luxury and assuring the public that recovery was just around the corner. Lessing, writing in 1968, accurately predicts the Watergate and associated scandals: "It was in the mid-seventies that it came out for how long the United States had been run by an only partly concealed conspiracy linking crime, the military machine, the industries to do with war, and government" (608). Indeed, large portions of this "fantastic" future fiction metamorphose, as the future depicted there becomes the recent past, into near documentary.

A second long letter from Martha to Francis tells how she survived the catastrophe—a nuclear holocaust touched off by mistake. Martha, now an old woman, lives an austere existence (which, in its primitivity and isolation from civilization's evils, appears almost utopian) with some seventy other survivors on an island off the coast of Scotland: she dies in the winter of 1997-1998. In the fifteen years prior to her death, she functions as the group's "Memory," and observes mutations in plant and animal life, especially the fact that many children born after the catastrophe possess extrasensory faculties. Martha suspects these clairvoyant children are "guardians" for the human race, whose knowledge is not endangered by insanity (like Lynda) or forgetfulness (like Martha). One particularly gifted boy, Joseph Batts, grows up under Martha's aegis and, upon her death, is sent to Francis in Nairobi. (He is, notably, like Amanda and her children, of mixed race—clearly, for Lessing the future will not be left in the hands of the white Anglo-Saxon.) Joseph Batts is the first of the "new children" (647), and will be followed by others in the *Canopus* novels. But Lessing also predicts here, for most survivors of the holocaust, an even more totalitarian and bureaucratic regime: "all humanity is passed, is cleared, is classified and subclassified into grades of purity ... governed by bureaucrats stratified on a world scale into 119 divisions" (650). The leftovers of the human race have learned little from the holocaust except to restrict personal freedom even more rigorously—a process to which even the rare emissary falls victim, at least for the time being. Joseph Batts, rescued from the island after Martha's death, is classified "subnormal" and "unfit for academic education" (649). This standpoint is one Lessing will revise, however, in *Shikasta*, where she depicts the same postholocaust phase in a more optimistic vein.

Many of the motifs, techniques, and ideas found in *The Four-Gated City* serve to build a bridge from the early works to the most recent space fiction. By developing the idea of an existential and physical totality which prevails completely independent of individuals, the novel paves the way for *Canopus in Argos's* later premise of quantum evolution for humanity. The idea of totality is underlined by the book's sundry epigraphs. All excerpts preceding the four parts—taken from Rachel Carson's *The Edge of the Sea*, Musil's *Man Without Qualities*, from science textbooks and writings on Sufism[9]—stress the impossibility of separating one substance from another. Moreover, they are united by the recurrent motif of water, not only one of Lessing's own oldest images, but the very constituent on which all living matter depends. Though still in rough-hewn form, the foundation of Lessing's later space fiction is visible already here, in the holistic concept of a thoroughly structured universe in which human beings need only recognize their rightful place. Lessing lends support to her heroine's belief that "tuning in" to this universe is a plausible, indeed vital procedure, by quoting the tenets of Sufism: "What ordinary people regard as sporadic and occasional bursts of telepathic and prophetic power are seen by the Sufi as nothing less than the first stirrings of [actual] organs . . . we have been given the possibility of a conscious evolution" (448).

Despite the obvious suitability of the quotation, Lessing denies that the volume "owed anything to

Sufism."[10] Indeed, the idea germinates in her early work with young Martha's belief that there must be a truer, more harmonious approach to life than most people suspect. Her vista of a conscious evolution is a final stage in the attempt to "remember" her harmony with nature and enter a plane higher than the one prescribed by convention. Martha Quest's consciousness thus not only reflects the author's increasing interest in universal wavelengths, but also prefigures Lessing's subsequent, still earthbound protagonists, who will depart from society's trodden paths and let themselves evolve inwards.

6

A Parcel of Well-Born Maniacs: Inner Space Fiction 1971-1974

The novels of the early 1970s mark another period of high productivity for Lessing, with three novels released in four years. Despite their closely spaced publication, they are extremely divergent in character, ranging from the joltingly cacophonic (*Briefing For a Descent Into Hell*) to the almost embarrassingly harmonic (*The Summer Before the Dark*). This dissimilarity indicates the author's resolute search for new fictional directions, once she had made her peace with tradition in the *Children of Violence* series. Preceding her investigation of outer space which was to begin in 1979, the three novels dealt with in this chapter investigate "inner space," that is, the subconscious, extrasensory, and "mad" realms. Lessing tests the viability of these routes toward a wholeness that can no longer be sought on the terms of the ordinary, everyday world.

Briefing For a Descent Into Hell

Published two years after *The Four-Gated City*, which has been described above as a pivotal point linking Lessing's early work to her mature production, *Briefing* is the portentous premiere of the second phase. It gives the reader a hint of themes and experimental techniques to come in the *Canopus* series, as well as a

foretaste of the vexation which is increasingly to domi-
nate the critical reception of Lessing's novels. Initial
reviews reproach the book for sluggish readability,
indecisive conclusions, and overreliance on the popular
radical psychiatry of R. D. Laing and others. While
considerably less palatable than its predecessor, *The
Four-Gated City*, its overall theme derives directly
from that novel: *Briefing* attempts an extended fictional
chart of the extrasensory wavelengths discovered by
Martha Quest. It turns into prose a state of mind that has
lost all contact with the external world. Lessing named
this intention on the frontispiece of the first edition:
"Category: Inner-Space Fiction—For there is never
anywhere to go but in." This maxim, interestingly
enough, is missing from the later paperback editions—
for reasons that will be discussed below.

The novel, like many of Lessing's narratives,
employs a frame. Charles Watkins, Professor of Classics at Cambridge, is found wandering the London
streets, suffering from amnesia and delusions. He is
admitted to a psychiatric clinic for transients, where
four weeks of extensive drug therapy have little effect
on his condition. The doctors X and Y eventually learn
his identity and piece together his biography from letters written by friends and relatives. When, after a
second month, all efforts to revive his memory fail, he
agrees to submit to shock therapy. This immediately
restores him to "normal," and he returns to his family
and academic duties.

Briefing is Lessing's first novel to use a male protagonist. While this fact is probably unimportant to the
author, who has never claimed to limit her scrutiny of
human behavior to one sex, it did not go unnoticed by
critics, some of whom, set free to call a man a man
again, overuse the word obnoxiously.[1] *Briefing* is also
the only novel in which Lessing uses clinical madness as
the major theme. Though all her characters theorize

about and dabble in madness, only Mary Turner and
Lynda Coldridge are mentally ill in the established
sense of the term, that is, consistently unable to cope
with everyday living. Characters like Anna Wulf, Martha Quest, and Kate Brown of *The Summer Before the
Dark* are temporarily immersed in the abyss of their
own psyches, but they are still able to deal strategically
with the outside world, and even fend off intruders if
necessary. The climactic mad phases experienced by
these heroines appear in retrospect as therapeutic sessions which restore sanity and renew psychic and moral
energy. Not so in *Briefing*, where madness demands to
be taken more seriously. Lessing's choice of a male
protagonist contributes to the book's force, since society
often stamps hysteria and irrationality as intrinsically
female traits. When males go over the edge, their condition cannot be dismissed as "the housewives' disease," a
cathartic vacation from humdrum routine.[2] Watkins's
insanity takes on drastic proportions—to the point
where "mad" reality competes for recognition with
"sane" reality and in many instances comes out the
victor. Thus the book must be read as Lessing's treatise
on the age-old question: who is madder, the sane or the
insane?

  While it has been pointed out repeatedly that the
book's structure and motifs are circular, its construction
is also bilateral or, to stay in the clinical context, schizophrenic. It juxtaposes the normal and the abnormal, the
astute and the deranged, the sane and the mad. Accordingly, it provides us not one but two protagonists.
"Patient," identity unknown, exists in the same body
with, but otherwise unrelated to Professor Charles
Watkins. Of the two, Patient (who clearly claims the
author's sympathy) is by far the more intriguing. The
first half of the book is set within his mind and is related
in stream-of-consciousness form. This, Lessing's first
major experiment with narrative technique, is a mor-

bidly captivating fantasy, laden with symbolism and images which merit repeated reading and interpretation.[3] The overriding theme of this interior monologue is the harmonious organization of parts into a perfect, many-faceted wholeness, expressed by images such as the web, honeycomb, crystal, soap bubble, polyphonic harmony, and so on. As the reader learns somewhat laboriously, Patient is drifting on a raft without an oar in the North Atlantic Ocean. His course describes an almost perfect circle, beginning off the coast of Northern Africa, reaching northward to the Azores and the coast of North America, ending finally on the shore of Brazil. Here he discovers the geometrical ruins of an ancient city. He attempts to clean and restore its crumbling square, actually a mandala or circle within a square, an ancient symbol of totality interpreted at length by C. G. Jung in *Man and His Symbols*. Patient's work is interrupted by the arrival of and ensuing brutal war between two animal tribes. One is apelike, the other a mixture of rat, dog, and human being, whose behavior reminds the reader most of the latter. This is the most memorable product so far of Lessing's grotesque fictional experiments with animal husbandry, a favored theme in her more recent works. The animals' bloody war is ended by the appearance of a giant white bird, a motif found in many fairy tales. Patient is lifted from earth by the bird, then by a "Crystal," foam from which he looks down on the planet and its inhabitants, tiny in relation to a huge universe: "the scurrying, hurrying, scrabbling, fighting, restless, hating, wanting little patches of humanity . . ." (100).[4]

A change of focus introduces an Olympian fantasy (clearly the by-product of Watkins's dealings with classical literature) in which Jupiter, Minerva, and Mercury puzzle over and meddle in human life below. The same scene is remade as science fiction when the space administrators Minna Erve and Merk Ury brief a team

of interplanetary emissaries for their descent to earth—
hell, indeed—during the last decades of the twentieth
century. (The conditions sketched here will be the
major focus of the later novel *Shikasta*.) Primary object
of these emissaries' mission is to combat the fragmentation of modern thought and restore to human beings
their "knowledge that humanity, with its fellow creatures, the animals and plants, make up a whole, are a
unity, have a function in the whole system as an organ or
organism" (128). Rather than a verbal briefing, the
emissaries are given "brainprints" and admonished not
to forget them. Lessing stresses once again the crucial
concepts of remembering and forgetting, important
not only as structuring leitmotifs in this and her later
novels, but also in the critic's decision whether to interpret events as lunatic fantasies or as actual—but
forgotten—realities.

With the brainprinting, Patient undergoes a rebirth
(prefiguring the narrator's reincarnation in *Shikasta*).
The scene is based on the pulselike repetition of the
word "sleep": "As the earth revolves, one half always in
the dark, from the dark half rises up a wail, oh I can't
sleep, I want to sleep, I don't sleep enough, but give me
pills to make me sleep, give me alcohol to make me
sleep, give me sex to make me sleep. SLEEP WELL"
(140). Sleep, an ever-present theme in Lessing's works,
has two major aspects. It can be a refuge when life is just
too much to face (as Martha Quest often retreats to her
bed when depressed). But it is also the source of inspiration and insight, where the subconscious is allowed to
quicken and speak. In analogy to Lessing's questioning
of the boundaries between sanity and madness, she
often reverses the dimensions of sleep and waking. Her
protagonists achieve their keenest wakefulness when
asleep and the average citizen, though superficially
awake, appears dulled and somnolent. Lessing laments
the human tendency to sleepwalk through life, fleeing
from rather than seeking acute, alert perceptions.

The scales are tipped from their balance between sleep and wakefulness when we are informed of Watkins's true identity—the book's structural turning point is reached here, at its arithmetical midpoint (p. 144). Stream-of-consciousness is now replaced by an eclectic mixture of dialogue, journal, letter-novel, and omniscient narration. The grand, shimmering, universal whole gives way to the pseudowhole in the form of the mental institution and its authorities, who now become Patient's antagonist. And Patient's fantastic world, of course, gradually recedes to let the "real" protagonist, Charles Watkins, come forward (despite Patient's refusal, to the very last, to believe that he has to be "Professor Thingabob" just because his biographical data say so). Patient's first exchanges with Dr. Y are classic examples of speaking at cross purposes. While the reader, being initiated in the context of Patient's sea voyage and briefing, understands exactly what he means, Dr. Y can only perceive his statements as totally deranged. Lessing places two realities side by side, each equally binding for its proponent:

> I am dreaming now.
> No, you are awake now. You are talking to me, Doctor Y.
> This is no different. A dream, like that.
> Oh yes it is different. This is reality. The other is a dream.
> How do you know?
> You'll have to take my word for it, I'm afraid.
> If I did have to, I'd be afraid. I can't take words for anything. (152)

Further exchanges are characterized by chronic ambiguities and the breakdown of language's potential to communicate. It is no accident that Watkins is by profession a philologist: his rejection of words as superficial and foreign to the truth (an insight gained by Anna

Wulf before him) reflects the disintegration of reality
itself. Thus, for him it is not a statement of the obvious
but rather an abysmal paradox when he laments, "I
gotta use words when I talk to you" (147). There is no
communication possible with words, since for him they
no longer correspond to anything real.

The "reality" elicited by Drs. X and Y through
letters and conversations is that Charles Watkins has
always been an outsider, enigmatic, and "above every
normal human emotion" (211). Nonetheless, he is irre-
sistibly charismatic to a select few, such as his admirer
Rosemary Baines or his mistress, Constance Mayne, in
whom he inspires the almost electrical need for wakefulness and clearer perception. Rosemary Baines perceives Watkins (and a parallel figure, Frederick Larson)
as the heralds of a finer and purer vision, which might
take humanity beyond the sense-dulling rituals of "reality" and the hopeless repetition of mistakes. She laments
that, despite the human race's never-ending hope to
improve upon itself, each new generation is corrupted
and sold pitifully short. The idea of unfulfilled human
potential is also the sustaining thread in Patient's journal, through which he is supposed to record his memories. A long episode recounts his underground work
with a World War II partisan group in Yugoslavia (actually not Watkins's own experience, but that of his friend
Miles Bovey, for whom the bell tolls early in the tale).
Partisan life appears as a frail, temporary, but perfect
utopia, for it allows a widely heterogeneous group to
thrive on idealism and unity of purpose, in harmony
with nature, "high and fine and foreign to the consciousness of ugliness of race or region or a hostile
religiosity" (234). It is a familiar irony that war—the
ultimate in stupidity and destruction—fosters the highest idealism and altruism in otherwise unexceptional
individuals. The partisan episode culminates in an
almost mythical assertion of the balance of life and

death, humanity and nature: Konstantina, the narrator's beloved comrade, is gouged and killed by a pain-crazed doe. Her silent burial in the forest loam is cele-brated by the rising of a newborn fawn to its wobbly feet: "perfect, a triumph." This scene has its counterpart early in the novel, when a female rat-dog is attacked and killed while giving birth, and the birth- and death-spasms merge into one.

Nature's inner harmony is also the subject of a second journal episode, describing the intricate move-ment of two plants, a camellia and a honeysuckle. They reveal to the narrator the importance of *timing* to all growth processes, and the perfection of their interac-tion illustrates once more Lessing's belief in the supe-riority of nature's laws, which prevail despite all human efforts to compartmentalize and classify. In an analogy established by nomenclature, the women who fall in love with the worldly Charles Watkins are named for abstract virtues (Felicity, Constance), but those who recognize his innermost self are named for plants—Rosemary and Violet.

A final episode involves Watkins's fatherly atten-tions to another mental patient, Violet Stoke, who embodies the book's division of proper surface reality from the unspeakable realms below. She appears in a high-necked, long-sleeved Victorian dress, the very essence of prudish and denied sexuality, were it not chopped off barely below the waist, deliberately exposing all that ample skirts are designed to cover. Inside the mixture of lady-plus-whore is a little girl, stunted in her growth by the terror of growing old and mediocre. The text implies that she, like Watkins, con-tains potential wisdom and clear vision necessary to penetrate the hypocrisy of civilized behavior—Lessing compares her to the figure who stares scornfully back out of a Goya painting. But Violet's intuition is nipped in the bud, defined as neurosis by a domineering family,

and she is left to wither in an institution, where her only
defense is the almost classical turning of her exposed
backside on the outside world.

Watkins, however, knows with increasing certainty
that there is something to be remembered. "There's
something I have to reach. I have to tell people. People
don't know it but it is as if they are living in a poisoned
air. They are not awake" (274). After undergoing shock
treatments, he indeed remembers, although, as the
reader must presume, he remembers the wrong thing.
He will probably return to his life as an elitist loner, who
lacks faith in his work, personal ties, and ordinary feelings. The scintillating journey inward will be relegated
to the status of a blown fuse, quickly replaced and
forgotten.[5] The interpretation of that voyage is left to
the reader, who has two basic choices. We can stick to
the novel's original maxim—that there is no place to go
but "in." If we do, Watkins's madness remains a fantastic internal landscape, product of an overworked imagination and comparable to other documented psychotic
ramblings.[6] Or, looking back from the perspective of
the *Canopus* novels, especially *Shikasta*, we can see
Watkins as harbinger of the author's incipient investigation of another "place to go": outward, toward an
external, all-encompassing picture of the universe and
humanity's history. The interpretation of Watkins's
journey inward as merely a first step toward the ultimate outward travels of Lessing's newest fiction is supported by the fact that *Briefing* prefigures many of
Shikasta's scenes. Most important is the correspondence between Watkins's anguished cry that he must
"remember," and an episode in the later novel during
which an emissary (who has forgotten the briefing for
his stay on earth and is thus in the midst of a mental
breakdown) is urged in his sleep by a visiting mentor:
"remember! Try and remember . . . I knew that what I
had fed to him as he slept would stay there and change

him. . . . He would remember. An enemy—for he was to be that for a time—would become a friend again, would come to himself."[7]

However we interpret Watkins's madness, the book stands as a polemic attack on orthodoxy: in psychiatry, in medicine, schooling, and interpersonal relationships. It assails inhumane psychotherapeutic methods, which countenance the sending of electric shocks through the human brain to force it into perceiving "reality" correctly. It also debunks formal education, one of Lessing's favorite themes. Watkins, representative of the elite educational establishment, begins his breakdown by rejecting scholarship as "hogwash." Academe is attacked as a major culprit in the compartmentalization of thought, stressing as it does oversimplified either/or constructions, while "it isn't either or at all, it's and, and, and, and, and, and" (150). The self-glorified pedagogical institution is humanity's oppressor rather than its servant, a fact Lessing illustrates with references to the cold and often inhuman architecture of schools and universities. Education, like psychiatry, pays lip service to individuality while applying every possible pressure to make the subject obey and conform. Through Watkins's experiences, the reader is "briefed" once again on the relationship between individuals (with their infinite, but usually smothered capacities), groups (institutions with exaggerated, dehumanizing authority) and "the whole," the dance of life, sound, and energy which Charles Watkins discovers during his sojourn with madness.

The Summer Before the Dark

The Summer Before the Dark is a further variation on the dialectic relationship between madness and normality, illustrated this time by pitting the protagonist against a single collective behavior pattern, the traditional feminine role-stereotype. In this novel, the organic, universal whole does not come into play. It is the only book in which Lessing gives dominant attention to the question of sex roles, which she sees in general as paltry compared to the other conflicts of our century. While many feminists welcomed the novel as a sign that Lessing was "finally" reassessing the feminist question, the text itself in fact proves exactly the opposite. The artificial sequestration of a feminist theme produces a work less compelling than those novels in which the sex war is only one of the protagonists' many conflicts. The book is nevertheless one of Lessing's most popular, so entertainingly readable that one could almost suspect the author of commenting, tongue-in-cheek, on the readers' tastes during the rise of popular feminism in the mid-1970s.

The novel expands what the story "To Room Nineteen" compressed into a nutshell, but leaves out the tragic ending. The protagonist here, Kate Brown, is a forty-five-year-old middle-class housewife and mother of four. She realizes one day to her surprise that she is no longer needed by her now-grown brood, nor by her debonair and unfaithful husband, nor by the household she has organized around them. She takes a summer job with the slick international corporation Global Food, which could (but doesn't) feed whole nations with the funds it squanders on public relations, administration, and entertainment. True to type, Kate falls into the role of nanny and hand holder for Global Food's delegates. At the end of the summer's duties, she travels to Spain with Jeffrey Merton, a twenty-five-year-old American, who promptly succumbs to an unspecified delirium. Kate leaves him in a rural convent and heads back to London, only to realize, once there, that her house is rented and she virtually cannot go home again. Now also in the grips of Jeffrey's existential fever, she takes a hotel room, where she lies near-comatose for days. When finally able to emerge, she is old—emaciated, wrinkled, and rat-haired. Her slow recovery takes place in a rented room with a young woman named Maureen. And a few weeks later, she is once more ready to go home to husband and family. Thus, the novel ends on an anticlimactic note comparable to the conclusion of *Briefing*.

Though Kate sees and criticizes the phoniness and injustice of the world at large, there can be no doubt that the large majority of her reflections are devoted to her role as wife and mother, in which she preserves the illusion of being needed by fussing perpetually over details. Her wifely status, product of the "archetypal" quest to find and keep a male partner, is characterized by "the light that is the desire to please" (243).[8] Kate has always put her own needs last, patiently holding the fort while her teenagers try their wings and her husband indulges in harmless little affairs. She stands by, a machine "set for one function, to manage and arrange and adjust and foresee and order and bother and worry and organise. To fuss" (94). In the course of the summer, she sees the feminine role she has played as a "web of nasty self-deceptions." It is flimsy, melodramatic, and as ultimately irrelevant as nineteenth-century theater (illustrated in one of Lessing's funniest scenes, when Kate publicly takes on the players of Turgenev's *A Month in the Country*). Well-adjusted, socially acceptable behavior appears to Kate (in her mad state) "as if a parcel of well-born maniacs were conducting a private game or ritual, and no one had yet told them they were mad" (155). In addition, she sees her own married life as a lie, gobbled up in bite-sized pieces by herself, a "fatted white goose."

The dimensions of the lie, however, become obvious only with age. Where a young mother with children is in fact needed, a middle-aged housewife often has artifi-

cially to create a demand for her services. The book
does not address feminine role-stereotypes in general
but rather their specific mutation and eventual crisis
conditioned by approaching middle and old age. The
"Dark" of the title, paraphrased as the "cold wind" of
the future, refers to old age; youth, accordingly, is
repeatedly characterized by warmth- and light-bound
imagery. The development of the old vs. young motif
hinges primarily on the question of appearance. Young
women are valued in our society for their looks, and the
fading of the youthful facade is—at least for Kate—a
major trauma. A young woman, says Lessing, "finds it
very hard to separate what she really is from her
appearance. . . . When you get a bit older . . . a whole
dimension of life suddenly slides away and you realize
that what in fact you've been using to get attention has
been what you look like."[9]

Using a compression of fictional time which is to
become more and more typical for her works, Lessing
lets Kate turn within a matter of weeks from a well-
preserved, still sensual woman to an eccentric old lady.
In the rapidity of this metamorphosis from young to old
lies the book's most artful aspect. Kate's development
appears as a two-story building with a trapdoor: above,
the comfortable suburban matron putters about,
patronized by neighbors and family; below is the emaciated hag with frazzled hair and ill-fitting clothes, who
is either ignored or given mistrustful, pitying glances.
The floor separating the two realms is loosely latched
by appearance and convention. It can, and does, give
way without notice, plunging Kate unawares to the
lower level.

Though Kate Brown provides a well-defined protagonist, none of the book's other figures is strong
enough to supply an antagonist. Her husband is a superficial philanderer, her children run-of-the-mill teenagers, whose affection is limited to an occasional con-

descending remark on the lines of "good-old-Mom." Mary Finchley, the neighbor who does exactly as she sees fit, symbolizes the total lack of Kate's need to please. But since this quality is developed strictly on the basis of her sexual promiscuity, she stands only for amorality and not for full-blown nonconformism. The people at Global Food are intentionally all poured out of the same mold. And Jeffrey Merton, while he prefigures Kate's approaching physical/psychic crisis, has no individual contours. Kate's antagonist is thus not personal but ideological: it is the feminine desire to gain the approval of others by fulfilling their expectations. While going through the motions of conforming for twenty-five years, Kate feels that her "real" self is suspended, a basket case waiting for a miracle cure. This is expressed in her repeated dream of the seal, a motif which makes this the crucial text for any study of dreams in Lessing's work. In her dreams, Kate is struggling to return the seal to water. It threatens to die if she can't carry it to safety, while she of course has no idea in which direction the sea lies. Like the waking Kate who must face the future's "cold wind," the dreaming Kate heads north on a Kafkaesque journey made progressively more difficult by snow flurries and the seal's increasing weight. Its pathetically stunted flippers and utter dependence on her pity make it a symbol for her own chronically dependent, stunted sense of self. When Kate is finally able to dream the last installment, in which she reaches the coast and returns the seal "full of life, and, like her, of hope" (241) to its own element, she can return home with a regained sense of identity. The seal disappears, indistinguishable in an ocean full of identical seals—a bleak outlook for Kate's anonymous future in the suburbs.

For if Kate feels miraculously purged of her need to please, she nevertheless returns to a spoiled family of five who are not freed of their need to be served and pacified. One doubts that they will shed their old habits as willingly as did Kate. The single most frequent complaint heard from the book's readers is that its conclusion returns Kate to the same old rut. Nothing has really changed, and we suspect she will remain "psychically jailed" and powerless to "resist the engulfing power of others."[10] This ending is, no doubt, truer-to-life than one wants to admit. It can also be argued in the book's defense that a radical change would be out of character for Kate. Her critical dissection of her own role results not from her desire for analysis and clarification, rather from the embarrassing insight that others now consider that role trite and obsolete. Had her family insisted that she was needed in London for the summer, the crisis would probably have been postponed or averted altogether. She is not the person to reject the trappings of a confining role *on principle*, but only when pragmatic considerations and wounded pride force her hand. It follows that her summer of role crisis, while it helps her understand the nature of her self-deceptions, does not revolutionize her personality. She returns "home," for better or worse. If the reader learns a lesson from Kate's adventures, it must be drawn from her (often astute) observations and not from her actions—she does not manage to set an exceptional or heroic example.

Because it focuses on feminine behavior without great regard for the social network which conditions role playing, the book often tends to bark up the wrong tree. It laments the fleetingness of youth rather than our youth-crazed society's brutality to the old. It reproves the woman who is desperate to please, but not the people who take for granted that an acquiescent female will always be at hand to deal with life's tedious details. Worst culprit in the latter category is Kate's husband, the book's most obnoxious and irritating figure, who however appears only very briefly. Kate's critique of the situation dwells on her own behavior and does not extend to the faults of her spouse. A good illustration of the novel's chronically misplaced emphasis is the humorous scene in which Kate, having discovered her "invisibility" to men when clothed in the guise of haggard old age, puts it to the test. When she strolls provocatively past a group of workmen, she receives a "storm of whistles, calls, invitations. Out of sight the other way, she made her small transformation and walked back again: the men glanced at her, did not see her. She was trembling with rage. . . . " (219). Kate rages at herself because she has spent her whole well-dressed and well-groomed adult life winning attention and admiration from men. She does not rage at the men for hooting and hawing, since she has always accepted that as "normal" behavior. One can safely say that she would never have questioned the premise underlying such behavior—the male right to assess every passing woman as a potential sex object—if circumstance had not rendered her suddenly "invisible" (i.e., old, skinny, and down on her luck). Her rage comes too late—and without clear recognition of the real enemy.

The only character apart from Kate herself to be drawn with strong contours is Maureen, a charming re-release of Julia Barr (of *Retreat to Innocence*). She has been called the "before" to Kate's "after":[11] all youthful energy and glowing health, she sees and dreads the capable-matron cum nagging-housewife existence which lies ahead, and clings for the moment to the tactic of abstention. She eats baby food and playacts, completing her roles with costumes and hairdos, all to avoid assuming a finite role—particularly the dowager's role she sees personified in Kate. Of the many suitors cluttering her doorstep, she is torn between Philip, proponent of a fascist youth movement which would restore decency, law and order, and old-fashioned patriotism to a society gone rotten; and William, an aristocrat who would sweep Maureen off to the pleasant pastimes of the landed gentry. The unhappy fact is, while Maureen wavers as to whom she will marry, she feels that marry she *must*. And the very status of marriage will trick her into becoming, like Kate, a bustling household-crisis manager. Vociferously she declares that she would do anything rather than assume this role, which she symbolically repudiates by cutting off her golden locks. A last stage in the novel's complex hair symbolism—it reflects youth and age, the need to please or the courage to displease—is reached when she weaves of her hair a little doll, the "bright fragile puppet" of compliant femininity. Though Maureen (unlike Kate) has not capitulated at the novel's end, the reader suspects the end is near—probably with William. Her future is inevitable and no number of baby-food meals can stave it off: "It doesn't matter a damn what you do. Or what I do. That is the whole point of everything" (242).

Of course, it is all very well for Kate and Maureen to spend weeks soul searching about their roles, since Maureen's parents foot the bill for her comfortable flat, and Kate still has some of the hyperbolic salary she received from Global Food. Their freedom from real material cares robs the plump exponents of the middle classes of a dimension which is present in Lessing's previous books: social awareness resulting from the fight for survival. We are reminded here for the first and only time of the heroines of Lessing's contemporaries, such as Margaret Drabble or Iris Murdoch, who are usually not burdened by mundane financial worries.[12] They are instead steeped in the identity crises which the better-heeled classes can best afford. *The Summer Before the Dark* demonstrates to the reader *ex negativo* what a crucial part the socioeconomic dimension plays elsewhere in Lessing's novels, setting them unmistakably into a class by themselves.

Which does not, of course, detract from the book's

message—that it is mad to accept society's standards of
normality at face value. And that unquestioning adop-
tion of prefabricated sex-roles may be enough to drive
even the sanest around the bend.

The Memoirs of a Survivor

Where *Briefing* charts mental breakdown and *The
Summer Before the Dark* examines role breakdown,
The Memoirs of a Survivor, hailed as "visionary" and
"bizarre," brings the inner space trilogy to a grandiose
conclusion by depicting the breakdown of Western
civilization itself. The novel shows the final collapse of
society's reference points and institutions, and thus
marks a caesura within Lessing's works. After this historical nadir, she seems to say, there is no longer any
point in grappling with "reality," which can't even be
salvaged, much less improved. Though realistic elements (such as spatial coherence and temporal causality) are still visible in this novel, at the time of its publication it was considered recklessly experimental. As it
inexorably proclaims the twentieth century's Ar-
mageddon, readers rightly wonder "where Lessing can
go from here."[13] Like Anna Wulf, who determines after
her madness that there is no place to go but up, Lessing
will assert, after this third traversal of the road inward,
that there is now no place to go but outward. Thus *The
Memoirs of a Survivor* can be seen as the end point in
the author's navigation of inner space en route to
wholeness, a final earthly station, described by a narrator who is already "imagining how things might be up
there in the higher regions, where windows admitted a
finer air" (6).[14]

Like the preceding two novels, *Memoirs* juxtaposes the inner and outer worlds. Both are overviewed
and related in the past tense by the Survivor, a nameless

elderly woman living in a moribund metropolis. Her narrative is chronologically structured by the maturing of Emily Cartwright, a twelve-year-old girl left mysteriously in her charge. The novel covers a span of approximately two years, leaving Emily fourteen at its conclusion. In the outside world, the narrator observes the decline of humanity from its once-civilized Age of Affluence to ever more primitive stages. The collapse is not due to any particular cataclysm, rather Western capitalist society simply rots from the inside out, as Marx predicted it eventually would. Both cause and symptom of the decay is the ever-widening gap between the exploitative, rich classes of "international administrators," and the masses, who can no longer expect even the most common daily amenities to function. Electricity and water supply are unpredictable and finally give out altogether. The cities gradually empty, as their citizens migrate to the country with vague hopes of finding something better. (In ominous analogy to the thousands of Jews who supposedly left their homes voluntarily to find "something better" in the Third Reich, no one has ever returned to tell the tale of the emigrants' fate.) Meanwhile, the metropolitan streets are taken over by hordes of looting youth. Street gangs turn into nomadic tribes who live by barter and foraging. With each passing day they come closer to unconcealed barbarism. Perpetual food shortage leads them to discard all taboos of civilization: house pets and rats, finally even human beings, are caught and roasted in the fight to survive.

In short, the events described by this captivating narrative are, with the exception of actual cannibalism, less visionary and "extraordinary" (as billed on the book's cover) than ordinary and all too familiar. They can be witnessed daily by many a city dweller in the Western world: administrative corruption at all levels, total bureaucratic confusion, faltering public services such as garbage collection, electricity and water supply; neighborhoods terrorized by gang rule. These scenes were the subject of many novels and films during the 1970s, and ultimately derive from the early 1960s, when England and consequently America were overrun by teen-age teddy boys and rockers. The scenario was popularized by Anthony Burgess's *A Clockwork Orange* and many similar novels.

Lessing's sketch of the near historical future stands side by side with the Survivor's subconscious world, which she enters by drifting "through the wall" of her living room into imaginary chambers. To put the thematic transition (made thirteen times in the novel) into a single phrase, it is the move "from Marx to Jung,"[15] that is, from historical to psychological evolution. The dissolving walls indicate the shifting borderlines between the "real" and the subconscious. In the world beyond the wall, the Survivor witnesses scenes from a childhood—presumably Emily's. These episodes have been described as "so ridden with the clichés of depth psychology that they could be packaged for educational television and labeled: Sibling Rivalry; Oral-Anal Regression; Sexual Tension between Father and Daughter."[16] The action behind the wall is intended to illuminate the origins of Emily's carefully "enameled," too-polite personality, and to mobilize the reader's sympathy for the misunderstood, helpless, belittled child. On the other hand, most readers will also sympathize with the parents, particularly the mother, a woman psychologically maimed by her efforts to adapt to "what society had chosen for her" (70). These parents are not malicious, only exhausted by the drudgery of child rearing and at a loss to communicate or even understand their own despair. Their terrorizing of Emily attests to the sad paradox that a child's psyche is often crippled worst by its parents' best intentions to raise clean, decent, "good" children.

The Survivor, observing the damaging effects of
excessive maternal guidance, refrains from mothering
Emily. She delves repeatedly into her subconscious
past, but does not try to influence the present through
parental edification (practiced dutifully by Martha
Quest on the Coldridge children). Instead, she relies on
"that hidden person in the young creature . . . the self
which instructs, chooses experience—and protects"
(58). Further attempts to "raise" Emily would only
intimidate or alienate her; and in any case, the hopeless
deterioration of surrounding society renders the usual
admonitions to grow up and take a responsible part in it
obsolete. While the Survivor's laissez-faire policy works
with Emily, whose moral sense is already formed, a
group of younger children will later bring the disastrous
disproof of her theory.

As the narrator herself observes, Emily is and
remains an anachronism. She is a symbol of the bourgeois past who grapples briefly but ineffectively with
the social problems of the present. The orderly world in
which Emily was born will be sacrificed to the ravages
of history before she is grown, just as the plush salons of
her childhood beyond the wall are repeatedly vandal-
ized and battered by unseen forces. But the portrayal of
Emily relies less on historical factors than on her personal, feminine role, as she attracts, admires, and wor-
ships her first love, then subsequently becomes disillusioned and embittered. Emily's personal development
structures the novel's six plot phases:

1. Emily alone (to p. 84)
2. Emily and Gerald (84ff.)
3. Emily and June (102ff.)
4. June and Gerald (142ff.)
5. Emily alone once more (169ff.)
6. Emily and Gerald reunited (213ff.)

The scheme is dangerously similar to the classic girl-meets-boy novel, and Emily's part in it is played out more or less according to that tradition. Her political self is sacrificed to her feminine career. She is in fact able (both in theory and in practice) to flourish in a social-democratic community, as she shows in the commune. But her social conscience is subordinate to her role as attachée of the commune's Führer-figure, Gerald. Even the narrator asks herself why Emily, who could become a leader on her own account, wants nothing more than to be the leader's "woman." When Gerald leaves the commune to proselytize among the cannibal children, Emily too immediately loses her sense of purpose there.

The archetype of feminine behavior acted out by "Emily the eternal woman" (171) is woefully traditional and undynamic. Like so many of Lessing's female characters, Emily has a chimeral womanhood sandwiched in between childhood and middle age (it can be precisely located on page 148). Though chronologically fourteen at the novel's conclusion, emotionally she is about forty, a "jaded woman of our dead civilization" (201). The final scene beyond the wall, in the chambers of Emily's past, shows her as a symbol of perverted, deformed femininity, a sex object in a vulgar strapless evening gown of 1950s vintage. She is "a grotesque" and is consumed, writhing and full of spite, in a puff of smoke: a fate well-deserved by the feminine cliché for which the doll ("ridiculous, both provocative and helpless") stands. But the clear-cut message of the individual scene lacks force, since the book on the whole fails to make clear the relationship of coy and degrading sex roles to the greater political patterns of dominance and submission. It also fails to develop any alternative to the feminine behavior that squelches Emily's élan vital and social idealism. Many minor details contribute to the book's implicit antifeminism. Of all the groups recruit-

ing on the pavements, it is the militant feminists who
spook away Emily's best friend, June. And the narrator
herself, who accepts as a natural consequence of the
situation Gerald's sexual appropriation and exploitation
of Emily (thirteen years old) and June (eleven), is dis-
quieted at the very idea of the two adolescent girls
sharing a bed.[17] Thus, while astutely singling out certain
damaging stereotypes, the novel perpetuates others—
not least through its tacit assertion that the sexist rituals
of romance-novel provenience are longer-lived than
nearly any other aspect of civilization.[18]

A deeper side of Emily is embodied by Hugo, her
faithful cat-dog, who suffers the chaotic decline of civilized behavior with anguished dignity. Hugo's pathos
reminds one of Kafka's verminized Gregor Samsa
(*Metamorphosis*), another vulnerable soul trapped in
distasteful animal guise. Hugo is in fact the novel's
noblest and most endearing figure. He stands for the
lost values of the old order: devotion, patience, loyalty,
sensibility, and courageous commitment to ideals. Of
course, in the dog-eat-dog world shown, Hugo's fine
feelings are just as anachronistic as Emily's femininity.
Her loyalty to him is her loyalty to an earlier way of life,
when the world was simpler and the rifts between
human being and noble beast could still be healed.

The juxtaposed forces of historical determinism
and the immutable subconscious cannot be reconciled
by a graceful conclusion. There is neither grace nor
mercy left in the Survivor's outer world, for which she
has "abandoned all expectations of the ordinary" (18).
Nevertheless, Lessing attempts to eclipse the external
dilemma through the force of consciousness: the magical parlor wall opens for a last time, and the few
survivors—the narrator, Emily and her parents, Hugo,
Gerald and his little cannibals—step out of reality and
into a metaphysical realm, where the mystical experience includes a brief glimpse of a female deity, "that

One who went ahead showing them the way out of this collapsed little world into another order of world altogether" (217). This solution does not plausibly reverse the historical and psychological inevitability built up in the preceding pages. The dilemma of persons caught between the jaws of a merciless late-capitalist metropolis (a dilemma real enough for millions, after all) cannot be resolved by a step into Nirvana. In *Memoirs*, Lessing has written an essentially open-ended novel but, refusing to relinquish her ties to tradition, retreats at the last moment to the sanctuary of a finite ending.

Its artificial resolution notwithstanding, the novel persuasively captures the fragility of civilization, which stands to lose thousands of years of progress within a single generation. Most children are not born with a moral sense, nor with a powerful "hidden person" to whisper right and wrong to them. The moment the older generations cease to set an example or fail to pass along their civilized ideals and restrictions, barbarism sets in. The Survivor's generation nevertheless feels unjustified in imposing their morals on a world that has outgrown them. Emily and Gerald, orphans of the capitalist Age of Affluence, manage a brief interregnum in a democratic commune, set up for homeless adolescents and deliberately organized without a power structure. But the collective fails: the children are unable to assume responsibility for the common good. On the contrary: they insist on setting Emily and Gerald up as authority figures, who must be there to dole out chores and apply pressure, but also must be rebelled against and finally deserted. While these adolescents abandon the communal experiment with nothing gained and nothing lost, they are followed by yet younger children who regress by several thousand years. Born and abandoned during the first migrations, they have no concept of civilized behavior. They live in averbal tribes in the sewer canals, feeding on rats and finally on human flesh. Wantonly killing and ravaging as soon as they are physically able, they are more destructive, more diabolic than the worst scavengers of the animal kingdom, and stand for the moral anarchy threatening all humanity: "It was terrifying ... those children were ourselves. We knew it" (181). Thus, in a reversal of the evolutionary scale, the animal (Hugo) stands for the highest "human" qualities in this novel, while the human child is a wild-eyed, amoral cannibal. In *Memoirs*, Lessing—like William Golding in *Lord of the Flies*—suggests that the steps backward into barbarism are few, and begin immediately when the young are left to their own devices. Her previous unflagging faith in the child now appears radically shaken. That these children cannot be domesticated is probably the single most striking proof of Lessing's new pessimism for the human race and its future.

This pessimism is further illustrated here by a radical denunciation of the collective or group mind. When the colossus of advanced civilization begins to stagger, humanity's immediate reaction is the formation of groups, gangs, and tribes. While the rare collective (such as Gerald's and Emily's commune) is inspired by an idea, most are simply a means to strength-in-numbers survival. Somewhere higher up, in the echelons invisible to the street people, are different collectives, formed and maintained for the purpose of exploitation: administrators, political bodies, police forces, propaganda organs. And lurking around the next corner is the final stage in degenerate mob behavior: a horde of bloodthirsty five-year-olds preparing their next lynching.

But *Memoirs* is not only a verdict on the perils of group behavior. The Survivor is also a last exponent of traditional, free-willed individuality, a concept that increasingly becomes subordinate to the idea of the whole in the forthcoming books. The devaluation of individuality already appears imminent here, for the protagonist as *individual* is stripped down to the bare essentials. She has no name, no age, no personal background, no profession. The details of her biography are reduced to the irrelevant. While she realizes she *could* act—leave the city, meddle in Emily's affairs—she does not. She already speaks comfortably in the "We" which is to characterize Canopus's archivists; like them, she records and observes events without attempting to intervene. In the context of Lessing's whole production, *The Memoirs of a Survivor* is most closely related to *The Making of the Representative for Planet 8*, and prefigures its theme twice (pp. 139 and 211). Both novels depict the irreversible crumbling of a life-sustaining order, endured and observed by a single narrative consciousness; both novels conclude with a mystical dissolution of the physical into the whole, proclaiming a new, harmonious unity (which the reader may or may not be inclined to accept). When the Survivor takes the step out of the "real" living room into the magical garden, the author steps away from the spent world of individual-bound reality into a whole which lies beyond. This will be the new direction of her next prose works.

7

This Is a Catastrophic Universe:
Canopus in Argos
Outer Space Fiction 1979-1983

The hiatus between *Memoirs* (1974) and *Shikasta* (1979), first in Lessing's newest novel series, is the lengthiest pause between major publications in her production since 1950. With the long-awaited appearance of volume one and subsequent rapid-fire publications of *The Marriages Between Zones Three, Four, and Five* (1980), *The Sirian Experiments* (1981), *The Making of the Representative for Planet 8* (1982) and *The Sentimental Agents* (1983), Lessing's readers found themselves confronted with a very different kind of fiction indeed, and forced to make an at least partial reassessment of the author. Critics were quick to distinguish "the old" from "the new," now apolitical and nonrealistic Lessing. And more than one reader has expressed the sense of having lost a friend with Lessing's abandonment of earthlings. Far from settling into the comfortable niche of "modern classics," these works are still unrelenting in their insistence that a new, more dynamic, less restrictive view of life must be pursued.

The author now shifts her focus from the entanglements and reflections of single individuals to the universe and its aeon-long evolution, both real and imaginary. She concentrates on an empire called Canopus that benevolently colonizes and administers many planets.[1] The one best suited to inhabitation is called

Rohanda or Shikasta—it is earth. All colonized planets are visited by Canopean emissaries, such as Johor and Klorathy, who descend like the mythological gods from Mount Olympus to observe, advise, and meddle. In Lessing's universe, Canopus stands for "good," that is, respect for the laws governing nature and history, whereas the rival empire Puttiora (ruling planet Shammat) is equated with evil, and the Sirian empire wavers between the two.

Many readers' first question is, of course, why this virtuoso of down-to-earth realism should turn to the fantastic at all. Several explanations come to mind. Science fiction eludes compartmentalized definition—it shares common ground with detective stories, fairy tales, scientific and historical documents, as well as many other genres—and thus appears well-suited to an author who progressively disdains the conventional demarcation lines between literary genres, between truth and fiction, the sane and the mad, the objective and the subjective. Further, the novels of the early 1970s attest to the fact that the artistic concept of realism, even in the term's broadest sense, is largely exhausted for Lessing. Its boundaries are too confining, and it is too political to accommodate her increasingly apolitical viewpoint. Like many ex-Communists of her generation, she no longer believes in literature as a consciousness-raising tool. Utopian fiction, in contrast, has two advantages.[2] While on one hand it provides escape from an altogether imperfect reality, it furnishes on the other hand a detached and often impartial perspective for scrutinizing the human condition. Since utopian scenarios—be they called Lilliput, Erewhon, or Zone Three—disclaim any connection to current events in real places, they are freed from the restraints of actual or self-imposed censorship. The writer who describes the distant universe or far-off future is free to say more—a fact well illustrated by the ideas in Orwell's

1984, which could hardly have flowered under the title "1949" (when the book was published). Lessing, who once said she was "tormented by the inadequacy of the imagination,"[3] now too gives her fantasies full rein. At the same time, she denies that her focus is substantially changed: "I see inner space and outer space as reflections of each other. I don't see them as in opposition."[4] And undeniably, her essential theme of the relationship between the individual and the whole remains constant, even if the whole involved assumes cosmic proportions.

Lessing now examines this question from the viewpoint of an intergalactic traveler and obtains results very different from those of the earlier novels. In *Canopus*, the whole consists of empires and planets evolving through the course of millennia, and assumes uncontested validity as good and right. Collectives (such as earthly political configurations) remain unchanged in their self-defeating and futile status. Individuals, however, are the big losers. They are no longer allowed to question authority—often they don't even know who this authority is, but they know it is to be obeyed. The space novels' continued concern with individual cogs as they fit into the larger pattern reflects once more Lessing's preoccupation with the dogma of communism. And ironically, her current verdict on individuality—requiring it to submit to the master plan at all costs—alludes to the fallacy that has plagued so many Communist collectives. For while communism aspires in theory to guarantee each individual equal rights and privileges, in practice personal rights are often sacrificed to the collective interest. Therefore, while Lessing may have come a very long way from her initial involvement in communism, the magnetism of its ideas—and pitfalls—is as evident in her works as ever.

Lessing has not said how many volumes *Canopus in Argos* will have, but at least a sixth volume is planned.[5] She emphasizes that the books are not necessarily meant to be read in sequence. For the purposes of interpretation, I will discuss volume 2, the series' black sheep, separately from the other volumes (which are loosely connected in style and theme). As a unifying motif in all the *Canopus* novels, one can single out the concept of *memory*, first introduced at length in *The Four-Gated City*. In order to preserve the "race memory" without which humanity can never evolve to a higher form of being, Canopus demands scrupulous documentation of all events in its sphere of influence. The books' comprehensive narrative frame is in keeping with the Canopean imperative "Remember"—they are all archives compiled by Canopus's historians, the "Chroniclers."

Shikasta (Volume One)

Re: Colonised Planet 5: Shikasta is the most formidable of the five *Canopus* novels to date. While it places stringent demands on the reader, it is indisputably one of Lessing's most intriguing achievements, if only for its complete disregard for literary precedent. The novel clearly aims at an analogical diagnosis of the ills of late twentieth-century civilization. This accounts for its "relevance" and popularity with readers born after 1960 (who frequently find *The Golden Notebook* dated and dreary). Due to its experimental nature, *Shikasta* is certainly not without weaknesses. The first hundred pages (which cover tens of thousands of years) are too ambitious in scope and at times make outright dull reading. Put in a nutshell, the history of the planet is as follows:

PRE-LOCK PHASE (lasting several million years). Rohanda, a swamp, gradually becomes life-sustaining. Canopus sets out to develop the apes

inhabiting it into a "Grade A species" within
20,000 years.

TIME OF THE GIANTS (begins 1,000 years after
colonization). Giants are hardy animals of Canopean stock, with a life span of four- to five-
thousand years. They are to be the planet's finest
specimens.

FORMATION OF THE LOCK (7,000 years after
colonization). A "Lock" is made between
Rohanda and Canopus, creating ideal conditions
for the giants, who are sustained by Canopean
strength called "Substance-Of-We-Feeling"
(SOWF).

FORCED GROWTH PHASE (7,000 to 17,000
years after colonization). The giants reach the
zenith of their evolution.

WEAKENING OF THE LOCK (17,000 years after
colonization). The failing atmospheric bond
enables Shammat, an empire representing evil
and corruption, to invade Shikasta and sap its
strength. Johor's first visit.

DEGENERATIVE PHASE Ice age (94f.), Rohanda flips over on its axis (97), deluge (99).[6]
Johor's second visit. He finds the Shikastan stock
severely degenerated, now with life expectancy
of only two to four hundred years. Since first
colonization, 48,000 years have passed.

CENTURY OF DESTRUCTION (20th century).
Johor's third visit, first incognito, then incarnated as George Sherban.

HOLOCAUST At the beginning of the twenty-
first century, one percent of the population have
survived the disaster and are rebuilding civilization.

Shikasta, not unlike *The Golden Notebook*, is
composed of bits, pieces, and fragments. The crucial

difference is that in the former, no apparent order is imposed on them—they are piled one upon the other in random layers, as historical documents often are. Five narrative categories, distinguished this time not by colored notebook covers but by typeface, fall into two major groups:

Historical Documentation:
1. Excerpts from historical volumes (boldface)
2. Johor's reports (roman type)
3. Interempire and top-secret official documents (small print)

Johor's Life as George Sherban:
4. Rachel Sherban's journal (italics)
5. Personal letters (roman)

For the purposes of analysis, categories 1-3 and 4-5 can be synthesized, providing on one hand a complicated account of Shikasta's history with emphasis on the latter half of the twentieth century; on the other hand, a traditional journal-novel, more or less complete with plot, protagonist, and denouement.

War is the recurring, dominant theme of the bold-face *History of Shikasta*. Twentieth-century Shikastans are "not aware that they were living through what would be seen as a hundred-years' war, the century that would bring their planet to almost total destruction" (85). The first two phases of this long war (known as World Wars I and II) pave the way for eventual annihilation by strengthening all industries involved in armament and chemical or nuclear warfare until they have absolute power over governments and populations. Shikasta's colossal war machinery stands in inverse proportion to the planet's dwindling ability to feed and house its population. Lessing concentrates especially on the privileged inhabitants of the few developed capital-

ist countries, who "forget" from day to day the broken
promises and gross errors of their administrations. They
are taught to live only for personal gain and accumula-
tion of wealth. These pages attack the ravenous consu-
merism characteristic of the post-World War II decades,
as well as the mentality of the "me generation" which
fails to see its part in the greater whole. The North
American continent is "heaped with waste, with wreck-
age, with the spoils of the rest of the world. Around
every city, town, even a minor settlement in a desert,
rose middens full of discarded goods and food that in
other less favoured parts of the globe would mean the
difference between life and death to millions" (90).
Ignoring the filth and pollution of their own countries,
as well as the deprivation in the Third World, the capitalist propaganda machines chant "more, more, more,
drink more, eat more, consume more, discard more"
(ibid.). Shikastans are driven and deceived by manipulative rhetoric, which is to become the main theme of
Canopus's fifth volume. They are unable to sort out the
contradictions of the mass media, which can sell them
literally any abomination in the name of democracy
and freedom.

But no amount of inflated PR slogans or Coca-Cola
can brake the Shammat-induced "degenerative disease." Its crippled victims turn to drugs, alcohol, or to
collective affiliations with nationalist, military, or ter-
rorist groups. A ray of optimism is shed on this hopeless
situation, however, by Lessing's treatise on nature. She
lauds the noble animal and plant worlds, which survive
despite the ravages of pollution. Again the tree symbolizes humanity's hope that nature might prove "stronger
in the end than the slow distorters and perverters of the
substance of life" (202). But here, as in *The Four-Gated
City*, nature can prevail only after World War III,
initiated by mistake, annihilates all but 1 percent of the
population. These few survivors can then be sustained

by the available SOWF, the Substance-Of-We-Feeling, and begin again on a cleansed and peaceful planet.

Johor, the Canopean emissary who has followed Shikasta's progress for millennia, observes the twentieth century with dismay. Lengthy case studies on both terrorists and envoys convince him that both are helpless to change the system, and at mid century he decides to embark on an earthly reincarnation himself, to try to halt the planet's degeneration from within. On page 210 he and Ben, a fellow emissary, are reborn as the twins Benjamin and George Sherban to enlightened British parents serving medical missions in Africa somewhere around 1960. A visual break in the text—two heavy black lines—initiates the story of Johor's further adventures, told primarily by the journal of his sister, Rachel. She has been instructed by a mentor to write down all her observations of George, in accordance with Canopus's obsession with record-keeping. Rachel and her parents have known that George is "special" since he was seven years old. While other children were learning Mother Goose rhymes, George heard voices and was visited by mysterious individuals (also reincarnated Canopeans, as we know). Both Rachel and Ben grow up devoted to George, who, however, does not emerge as a clear-cut positive figure. Rachel is in fact the heroine of her own journal, and her fate is far more involving for the reader than her brother's. George becomes a charismatic leader of youth gangs, then in international youth organizations. By the time he reaches adulthood, the superbureaucratized world governments have been consolidated into a collective dictatorship, "The Pan-Europe Federation of Socialist Democratic-Communist People's Dictatorships for the Preservation of Peace." In the name of this peace, apparently, both Sherban brothers are put on the extermination list, and Rachel, disguised as George in hopes of throwing his pursuers off the track, is killed.

Letters tell the rest of the story. George and Ben take
part, shortly before World War III, in an apocalyptic
mock trial of the white race, held in Zimbabwe. The
trial fizzles out with the insight that man's inhumanity to
man is universal, a laconic outcome typical of these
novels' shoulder-shrugging indifference to political
issues. Shortly thereafter, Benjamin Sherban dies, after
he has helped to save the "special" people sent to him by
Lynda Coldridge. After the holocaust, George works
on the rebuilding of civilization, now unwarring and in
harmony with nature, and soon dies, since his—that is,
Johor's—mission is accomplished.

Kassim, a child adopted by Rachel before her
death, is the "new man" who grows up in an earthly
Eden. He sees built up around him a brave new civilization, symbolized by geometrical architecture. The new
cities are scalloped, octagonal as well as star-shaped
(only a pentagon appears to be missing). With the
theme of architecture Lessing not only alludes to her
own work—such as Martha Quest's four-gated vision
and Charles Watkins's discovery of geometric ruins—
but to a theme as old as Thomas More's *Utopia*, where
the cities were quadratic.

With this prophecy of civilization's rebirth ends the
first and most ambitious installment of *Canopus in
Argos*. It is not a homogeneous book, and the reader
takes into the bargain a fragmented construction, occasional pathos and sentimentality, and passages which
are boring, confusing, or both. Moreover, certain
aspects of *Shikasta* foster a deep apprehension (which
will be borne out by the coming volumes). First, Canopus's genetic manipulations remind one all too clearly
of Nazi Germany's aspiration to breed a superior, purer
race. Second, the book tacitly asserts the privilege of
empires to expand and colonize—a process which Lessing observed, with all its concomitant monstrosities, in
her twenty-five years in Africa. And finally, *Shikasta*

requires its figures to bow to authority, as Rachel, Ben, and hundreds of disciples blindly obey George, and as Canopean emissaries obediently carry out their orders. The inhabitants of Lessing's new universe have no free will, a factor that will keep many readers from taking the books seriously. In short, this and the following volumes of *Canopus* depict totalitarian systems but neglect to question the premises on which they operate.

The Sirian Experiments (Volume Three)

The third volume of *Canopus in Argos* is also presented as a report, written this time by a Sirian "female bureaucrat"[7] named Ambien II. It covers the same time period as does *Shikasta*, from the first colonizations, through the formation and subsequent failure of the Lock, culminating in the Century of Destruction. Sirius's part in Rohanda's history is as follows: After traditional rivalry and finally the Great Sirius-Canopus War, these two empires enter a truce which ends hostilities. Sirius shares Canopus's interest in experimental breeding and evolution, and is granted use of Southern Continents I and II (Africa and South America) for experimentation. Sirius's experiments are not successful and eventually are reduced to "minimum performance."

Ambien II is one of Sirius's five dictators, and has been in the Colonial Service for aeons (Sirians do not die, since their parts are replaced as they wear out). Though technologically further advanced, the Sirians recognize Canopus's superior wisdom, ethical sense, and judgment. Sirius is hampered by lower emotions (greed, false pride) as well as by the desire for quick and unambiguous profits in its endeavors. Thus Ambien is placed for the duration of her dedicated work on Rohanda under the guidance of the Canopean emissary Klorathy, who tries to teach her (and thus her empire) respect for the inner laws governing the universal clash of good and evil. Ambien's task is to enlarge her perspective regarding the necessity of this clash, since her pragmatic Sirian inclination is simply to blast the evil or unwanted elements off the map. As she becomes more and more committed to Rohanda, Ambien is estranged from her four codictators, who have written the orb off as an unprofitable investment. Finally, she is exiled on planet 13, where she writes her report.

Not unlike the jailed Galileo, Ambien has to smuggle her treatise off planet 13 and into circulation on the mother planet. In keeping with the series's overall theme, she is determined to do this for the sake of memory. She sees her report as an "attempt at a reinterpretation of history" (8) meant to revise Sirius's understanding of events on Rohanda. Hindsight-is-insight is therefore the book's major leitmotif: "looking back" (11); "we know now" (14), "what I see now, looking back" (57), and so on. This Wonder Woman, whose mechanical reflections admittedly cannot compete with the intellectual and emotional agonizing of Lessing's earlier heroines, has her most "human" quality in her determination to learn clearer vision and attain a "change of viewpoint" (273).

Ambien's education involves three episodes placing her in mortal danger, which take place in the cities of Koshi (possibly Persian), Grankonpatl (Aztec) and Lelanos (Central or South American). In all three situations, she is accompanied by a Canopean tutor, either Klorathy, Nasar, or Rhodia. The purpose of these brushes with death is to make Ambien reflect on the concept of mortality and eventually see her own individuality as relative rather than absolute. Thus, throughout her report, she gives a running commentary on individuality (echoing in part the author's Preface to the book): "Each person everywhere sees itself, thinks of itself, as a unique and extraordinary individual, and never suspects to what an extent it is a tiny unit that can exist only as part of a whole" (272). But in order to smoothly integrate itself with this invisible whole, the individual must first resist the collective or "group mind," a concept present in Lessing's work since *Martha Quest* and developed at length in *The Four-Gated City*. Group minds are highly manipulable and can be programmed to overlook even the most obvious truths. A collective plugged in to a group mind is ruled by mob spirit, prejudice, and cowardice. Modern group minds are fed and maneuvered by the mass media but become, at some point, self-propelling. As the individual is bent by the surrounding group mind, Ambien proposes that enlightened individuals (like herself) must induce mutations in the existing pattern. Deviant thinkers may be ostracized and labeled insane, but eventually they will enjoy the distinction of having seen the obvious in time. Ambien takes her banishment tranquilly, musing that the other four may one day join her in corrective exile. She is unique among *Canopus's* protagonists in that she manages effectively to question and counter the prevailing group spirit. As a result, she is temporarily robbed of her life's purpose as envoy to Rohanda, but at least she is no longer in the service of ideas she considers false. Ambien's rejection of the group in the name of a greater good makes her a parallel figure to Martha Quest, who also repudiates collective identities and roles, retains only vestiges of her original qualities in long exile, but eventually gains touch with a wavelength she perceives as whole and true.

Though these central ideas worked out by Ambien are illuminating and thought-provoking per se, *The Sirian Experiments* on the whole lacks coherence and sustaining force. In a potpourri of aphorisms, digressions, and adventurous episodes, readers miss a "human dimension"[8] as well as a clear analogy to the here and now. There is no meaningful temporal nexus, since the action bounds haphazardly between various (mostly prehistoric) centuries. An additive structure randomly piles up bizarre and grotesque episodes. Ambien witnesses the rise and fall of dozens of weird species; she is incarcerated and barely escapes bloody sacrifice at an ancient Aztec altar; she inhabits the body of a queen killed by Mongols. Later she witnesses gruesome experiments performed on living subjects, justified by a "scientific interest" comparable to that of Nazi Germany, in the belief that beings "of an inferior kind did not feel physical or psychological pain" (223). Readers will be irritated, to say the least, by Ambien's cold-blooded refusal to interfere with such barbarism. It is all just part of her education regarding the battle of good and evil.

Corruption is again represented here by Shammat, the planet which leeches Rohanda's strength. Shammat's emissary is Tafta, a ruthless opportunist, who reaches his zenith when incarnated as a charismatic "senior technician" working in America. His function is to spout propaganda to the effect that pollution, radiation, nuclear and chemical wastes are really innocuous to the general public's health. Doubters are ridiculed and finally silenced by the Shikastan "group mind," so strong that most earthlings cannot bear the shame of having an original thought. Following his successful speeches, the devilish Tafta rubs his hands with glee: his assignment has been to test the "imperviousness among these Rohandans to the truth of their situation . . . it is absolute" (281). Nevertheless, Canopus believes events on Rohanda will take their right and necessary course: when Ambien meets Nasar for the last time, on a hilltop overlooking a smog-covered metropolis, he admonishes her from behind his gas mask to "remember" that Canopus does not "deal in failure."

Bearing in mind that an author is not necessarily the best critic of her own works, we should cite Lessing's statement of intention. She calls *The Sirian Experiments* a "direct result of nearly fifty years of being fascinated by the two British expeditions to the Antarctic led by Robert Falcon Scott."[9] She has written a long commentary on those expeditions and their importance to this novel. The analogy is indeed, as Lessing suspects in deference to her too "casual, or literal-minded"[10] readers, not immediately evident, since *The Sirian Experiments* fails to develop it clearly. Lessing sees in the South Pole expeditions the paradigmatic transcendence of a chaotic world (at the time in the throes of preparation for World War I) to pursue a noble, scientific feat which tested the world's very horizons. All Arctic expeditions were characterized by almost superhuman and certainly supernational efforts at scientific erudition, which took no notice of external hardship. Until their deaths, explorers such as Scott and Edward Wilson not only clung to their goals, but wrote detailed journals—believing, like Lessing's Canopeans, that humanity's crucial moments must be accurately recorded. Ambien, too, dutifully records the process of her growing consciousness and survival instinct, as she learns to see beyond the physical: "Now I was thinking that if I was worth a survival of physical extinction, then what there was in me to survive, would—*must*" (218). Ambien's evolution reflects the essence of the search for the South Pole—the human need, often paid for by "madness," hardship, exile, even death, to cross over boundaries into new realms with larger perspectives. That this idea emerges so weakly in *The Sirian Experiments* has mainly to do with the choice of protagonist: it is hard to infuse human passions into a million-dollar robot with a lifetime guarantee, who crosses borders not on snowshoes but in a space bubble. Lessing will return to the themes of *The Sirian Experiments* with a more human viewpoint—and an analogy conspicuous enough for the literal-minded—in the fourth volume of *Canopus in Argos*.

The Making of the Representative for Planet 8 (Volume
Four)

Shortest and most concisely constructed of the
Canopus novels thus far, *The Making* was conceived by
Lessing as a tangible demonstration of the abstract idea
underlying its predecessor, that is, the testing of human
powers to survive, transcend, and forge new viewpoints. The earlier novel's currents are grounded here in
a single minisociety, Colonized Planet 8, whose lamentable fate was mentioned by Ambien in passing.[11] In the
clearly human appeal of its characters and the linear
simplicity of plot, *The Making* is more readable than
either *Shikasta* or *The Sirian Experiments*. It is both a
fantasy on the rise and decline of a race, and an allegory
of the battle between hope and despair in the face of
catastrophe—at any time, under any circumstances.

Planet 8, of Eden-like climate and beauty, is used
by Canopus to harbor a species evolved through syn-
thetic breeding. These people live in preindustrial harmony, each village distinguished by its special trade.
Hardship and discord are foreign to Planet 8, as is the
concept of free will. The race's essential functions
(herding, teaching, agriculture, etc.) are guarded by
Representatives. Doeg, the "Memory Maker and Keeper
of Records," provides the account given here. He describes how the people are instructed to build, under
Canopean supervision, an impermeable black wall
encircling the planet. Shortly after its completion, snow
(next to unknown in the mild climate) begins to fall.
This is not an unusual application of a common motif—
snowfall in literature often portends existential crisis
and imminent disaster. Planet 8 gradually moves into an
ice age, but the people hold out because Canopus has
promised to save them by space-lifting them to Rohanda.
Atmospheric and physical stress undermines their moral
energy; after a period of criminality and violence most
of them sink into lethargy. When Johor finally arrives

from Canopus, he dashes their hopes of rescue. Rohanda
has become unfit for migration through the degenerat-
ing Canopus-Rohanda Lock, and those inhabitants of
Planet 8 who have not already starved or been buried
alive by snow slowly freeze to death. Without the
slightest prospect of surviving, the collected Representatives trek northward through the blizzards until they
freeze to death on a mountaintop. Then occurs "the
making": with their physical deaths, their conscious-
nesses are fused into a single, transcending unity, "the"
Representative for the planet, whatever its future might
be. The vast, landscapelike prose describing the cata-
clysmic glacier can be counted among Lessing's finest
narrative achievements—a tour de force that is utterly
chilling to read.

The book's point of departure is identical to that of
volume two, *The Marriages Between Zones Three,
Four, and Five*: a world previously harmonious and
orderly suddenly ceases to function properly. In both
cases, though things fall out of phase through no fault of
the citizens, their response to the crisis is not to question
or rebel, but to become even more obedient and servile
to Canopus's decrees. Where *Marriages'* Zones are
saved by strategic missions across their boundaries,
Planet 8's crisis has to be met from within by idealism
and resourcefulness. First fed by illusion (since they
don't doubt Canopus's promise of rescue), but then
without any glimmer of hope or even the comfort that
their suffering is in a good cause, the Representatives
personify the will to survive. They continue all efforts
to save the starving herds and the planet's dwindling
vegetation even after the majority of the population has
retreated to await death in their inundated huts. Hopes
are hinged for a time on a magical plant (a motif developed further in the series' next volume), which is har-
vested and stored in the freezing lakes and rivers, to be
eaten in icy chunks during the winter. The theme of

survival instinct was developed at large in *The Sirian Experiments*, but the Representatives for Planet 8, not Ambien II, are the first to give it contours and depth. Their situation brings home to the reader not only the colossal power of the elements, but also the extent of human endurance. It is interesting to note that Lessing, commenting in a 1982 interview on humanity's survival instinct, cites ice ages as the real test of strength[12]—after all, the last glaciers retreated only eleven thousand years ago and, in Canopean time-spans, the next Pleistocene is just around the corner.

To demonstrate this point, *The Making* makes no concessions to a conventional time framework. In the context of a race's greater evolution, our petty sense of hours and years is irrelevant. Like a high-speed projector, the book shows, for instance, some pet martens who are all plump and playful health one moment, but sicken and die within the course of a brief conversation. Time flies ever faster as the end approaches: the Representatives are called in midwinter to the temperate zone, now only a few miles wide, where it is "summer." Even as they arrive there, the blotches of vegetation wither, frost covers the ground, and shortly the blizzards begin once more. Objective time has lost its value, as has the objective locus: snow submerges villages, Planet 8's ocean, the monolithic wall and finally the mountaintops. Accordingly, the Representatives (except for Doeg, who must write it all down) lose their functions and thus their individual identities, since there are now no herds for the herdsmen, no fields for the grower, no children for the teacher. The transcendent "making" is preceded by an absolute loss of individuality. Thus, in Lessing's specific application of the utopian novel, she not only relies on an imaginary time and setting, but lets these elements self-destruct by the novel's conclusion, taking with them the now obsolete concept of the individual.

The author's "Afterword" to the novel, mentioned above in connection with *The Sirian Experiments*, describes at length her inspiration by the expeditions to the Antarctic in the early twentieth century, particularly Robert Scott's belated discovery of the South Pole and subsequent death. A similar historical dilemma immediately springs to mind—the fate of Germany's Sixth Army at Stalingrad during the winter of 1942-1943, when it froze and starved to death, sustained only by the empty promises of pending supplies and reinforcements. These analogies lend extra strength to the book's examination of human consciousness when isolated by a foreign element from reality, external support, and finally from hope itself. Lessing sees the biologist and explorer Edward Wilson as the South Pole expeditions' "moral focus" and as a Chronicler when record keeping was of the essence—the last days of the explorers' lives are known only through faithfully kept journals, which were recovered months after their deaths. Once again, Lessing—though she does not always take time to make clear the exact connections between Planet 8, the South Pole, and the "Spirit of History"—points out that humanity's climactic moments, especially its mistakes ("holocausts, famines, wars, and the occupants of a million prisons and torture chambers" [126]) cannot be dismissed as unavoidable blunders if ever progress is to be made.

Unlike the slow and grinding progress of the human race, however, there seems to be little sense in Planet 8's bitter end. The virtues of high-minded idealism notwithstanding, it will not feed fires and fill empty stomachs. Even if Canopus regards death as merely a "change of circumstance,"[13] it might have evacuated Planet 8's population to Rohanda, which, despite the failure of the Lock, still has thousands of life-sustaining years to go. But such arguments are pointless, since Canopus, here and in the other novels, never justifies its

actions. As in *Marriages*, the reader is asked at the end to
take it on faith that something better has been achieved
and the strain purified. The existence of the chronicle
itself (i.e., the fact that Doeg the Memory Maker saw a
point in writing it all down for the archives) provides
the circular hermeneutic "proof" that the race's downfall was to a greater purpose. Doeg undergoes a mystical revelation at the book's conclusion, when he realizes
that literally every atom of the frozen planet still has its
unique place in the whole. Substance is not destroyed
but transmuted; one pattern of matter may have been
reassimilated by the physical substance of Planet 8, but
it is replaced by another that is "every bit as valid and
valuable as what we had known as real" (120). Valid for
the Representative—not necessarily valid for the hundreds frozen stiff beneath the glacier.

  The Making, despite its catastrophic content, is
typical for the "new optimism" of Lessing's later
works—an optimism founded on fantasy rather than
fact. In tone and message it reminds one of the earlier
novel *Memoirs of a Survivor*, and can be seen by the
inclined reader as another work in Lessing's "mystical"
tradition, since it both culminates in the "allness"-vision
typical of nature mysticism, and assuages the pains of
the here and now by suggesting their correspondence to
some greater, transcendent reality: "we do not often
enough wonder if our lives, or some events and times in
our lives, may not be analogues or metaphors or echoes
of evolvements and happenings going on in other people . . . in this world of ours or, even, in worlds or
dimensions elsewhere" (145).

The Sentimental Agents (Volume Five)

*Documents Relating to the Sentimental Agents in the
Volyen Empire*, whose title is totally in keeping with its

lackluster style, treads familiar ground in many respects. Like the other *Canopus* novels, this most recent one describes the adventures of Canopean agents as they are trained for duty in the universe. Again we are dealing with an empire, this time consisting of four planets: Volyenadna, Volyendesta, Maken, and Slovin.[14] Events in their history are not unlike those described in *The Sirian Experiments* and *Shikasta*: species evolve and decline, territories are conquered and subjected to colonial rule, native populations are enslaved and tyrannized. The interplanetary action of *The Sentimental Agents* is quickly described: both Volyenadna and Volyendesta are about to be overrun by Sirius (which has fallen into total disorder since the demise of the Five). It is the mission of Klorathy (whom we remember as Ambien II's tutor) to see that acts of aggression are averted without undue violence. He prevents the first invasion by supplying the Volyenadnans with a magical plant, Rocknosh, which makes them self-sufficient and therefore immune to tyranny. Volyendesta is then invaded by the neighboring planet Maken, but through Klorathy's timely instruction in passive resistance, the citizens are able to inspire in their conquerors a change of heart.

Once more, the emissaries' education runs parallel to the planets' evolution. Klorathy's reports relate the trials of the erring young envoy Incent who, though he reappears regularly and is apparently intended to be the protagonist, never really takes on personality. Incent is in danger of losing the objectivity of his Canopean briefing and is, instead, infected and intoxicated by words. In the novel's terminology, he suffers from "Undulant Rhetoric," a disease called by a simpler term in *The Golden Notebook* when Anna Wulf compulsively plays the game of "naming." Both characters suffer from the quixotic delusion that words can contain truth. Despite Klorathy's efforts to reprogram

Incent, he backslides stubbornly and at the book's conclusion has made no progress.

With Incent, Lessing improvises on literary tradition. The theme of the individual who deviates from the
"party line" is one of the oldest components in utopian
novels—one is reminded of Zamiatin's *We*, of Orwell's
1984, of Bradbury's *Fahrenheit 451* or of Huxley's *Brave
New World*. In these novels, the aberrant protagonist
fails to absorb propaganda and instead forges a critical
viewpoint which becomes the focal point of the narration. Through this partisan hero, the brutality of the
greater social machinery is exposed. Exactly the opposite effect is achieved by Lessing's protagonist. He dis-
tinguishes himself not by repudiating but by embracing
propaganda to which he was supposed to remain
immune. Because he believes in the persuasive power
of words as a means to enlightenment and liberation, he
is considered a reactionary and a fool. Big Brother
Klorathy, on the other hand, is indeed watching, and
represents the moral force which might guide him back
onto the right track.

Incent's illness sums up the target of the book's
polemics: the illusory nature of words. They appear as
the enemy of rational action and human progress.
Words infect and derange the human mind; slogans
incite to mob spirit, revolution, and war. They lead to
emotionalism and sentimentality, and prevent people
from doing the right thing at the right time, that is, from
observing what Canopus calls "Necessity." In an attempt
to illustrate the atrocious and destructive power of
phrases, Lessing cites an historical example—the French
Revolution. It appears here as the epitome of rhetoric-
incited violence and stupidity. When an oratory-infected
agent fails to respond to all other treatment, he is given
"Total Immersion" and transported backward in time
to relive the Revolution as a French worker. He survives
the *terreur* in Paris, only to die of starvation with Napo-

leon's armies two decades later. After unspeakable tortures, he sees that the Revolution, with all its grandiloquent brilliance, has been to no avail. Insight achieved through "Total Immersion": revolution is senseless, its perpetrators maddened by lofty phrases, the masses slaughtered but for empty words. A sad verdict indeed, from an author who once so eloquently supported the ideas born with the French Revolution and encouraged rebellion against the forces of oppression. The book strays far from reality (for rhetorical purposes!) in its proposition that revolutions take place and fail only because of nasty rabble-rousing slogans. Historically speaking, they take place because of the oppression of the many by the few, and some actually have failed because the many were too slow—not too quick—to verbalize their plight, revolting only when all economic resources were depleted.

As opposed to the quasi-historical documentation offered by the French Revolution, the book's concluding episode provides a hypothetical example for constructive resistance to rhetoric. Inhabitants of Volyendesta have been united in "defend ourselves to the death" patriotism by the eloquent leader Ormarin. They are determined to repel the pending invasion of Makens, who arrive on winged saurians called pipisaurs, from whose "secretions" they feed (this pun doubtlessly can be ascribed to the "broad humor" promised by the dust jacket). Klorathy arrives first, however, to prepare Volyendesta to accept and make the most of the inevitable. He convinces them to abandon their belligerent territorial instincts, greet the invaders graciously, and invite them to remain as guests. This brilliant tactical scheme so disorients the Makens that they eventually go home again, leaving only a small occupying force, which is then assimilated into an already heterogeneous population. After all, the invaders and the invaded cannot help but see "how

absolutely like each other they are" (175). Conclusion:
through passive resistance to heated rhetoric and group
emotions such as militant patriotism, a happy ending
for all will be achieved. A thesis for which, unfortunately, historical evidence is lacking, since few conquerors are so easily thrown off the track as the sim-
pleminded pipisaur-riders.

Under the general heading of rhetoric-induced
behavior, Lessing illustrates many mechanisms motivating both the masses and their politicians. Uniting the
two is their Pavlovian readiness to resort to violence,
while admitting they do not know who the attacker is or
even why they're fighting. Similarly, she levels her
sharpest attack to date on Christianity, "one of the most
savage and long-lasting tyrannies ever known even on
that unfortunate planet [Shikasta] . . . which allowed no
opposition of any kind, and kept power by killing,
burning, torturing its opponents" (100). Religious fervor, responsible for the slaughtering of thousands in the
name of piety and salvation, serves to illustrate once
more the power of mob spirit or "group minds." In a
court scene reminiscent of both *Shikasta*'s trial of the
white race and the satire on jurisprudence in *In Pursuit
of the English* (where it was done more wittily), the
governor of Volyen brings suit against the entire empire
for concealing from the population their real nature as
group-determined beings. The main idea emerging
from the sprawling discourses on group behavior is that
most human beings are conditioned to need a tyrant,
since they feel most comfortable when oppressed.

This premise was first developed in studies such as
Wilhelm Reich's *The Mass Psychology of Fascism*[15] and
Erich Fromm's *Escape From Freedom* (1941). Lessing
demonstrates it when Incent, in the grips of rhetorical
fever, travels to the planet Slovin to persuade its inhabitants to become democratic and resist tyranny. The
audience is so enthused by his rhetoric that it turns into a

mob and demands that he become their ruler—he barely escapes being crushed by a throng of fans. He has failed to make clear to his listeners that they must abandon the pack instincts of their all-too-recent animal past, in which "everything that will conduce to the survival of the group is an imperative . . . while outside are enemies, who are *bad*, to be ignored if possible, threatened if they intrude themselves, destroyed if necessary" (99; emph. orig.). The nationalistic masses yearn for a despot as a wolf pack yearns to follow its leader. The only difference is that the human leader can manipulate the followers through rhetoric and commit atrocities at will in the name of Liberty, Virtue, and Democracy. He can starve the populations while arming them to the hilt, spoon-feeding them the absurd contradiction that armament is the tool of Peace and Prosperity. Both rulers and subjects appear as victims of that deadly weapon, rhetoric.

An important interpretive aspect of *The Sentimental Agents* lies in the dialectic and sometimes controversial relationship of its central ideas to their counterparts in earlier works—the theses developed here attest indeed to the author's own rapid and unpredictable evolution. The book retracts or reverses many of Lessing's earlier tenets, starting with the epigraph for her first novel, *The Grass is Singing*, which declares that the outcasts of any society are the most poignant indicators of its weaknesses. In the 1957 essay "The Small Personal Voice," Lessing suggests that the temporary dejection among liberals and socialists in the 1950s could be lessened, their optimism restored "by comparing our times with the disillusionment which followed the French Revolution." The same motif has, in this newest novel, exactly the opposite effect. Incent, whom we first encounter in the infirmary, also reminds one of Charles Watkins (*Briefing*), another maverick who had to be forced back into conformity by drastic measures.

But where the treatment given to Watkins—"Total Immersion" in drugs and finally shock—was depicted as barbaric and ignorant, Incent's "therapists' " right to rehabilitate him is uncontested and apparently outweighs his individual right to differ. Finally, this protagonist's situation presents a marked contrast to characters as recent as Ambien (*The Sirian Experiments*), who, unlike Incent, is at least allowed to reject her briefing with dignity. These are but a few examples which serve to illustrate the volume's importance as a reference point in the greater development of Lessing's views.

   The Sentimental Agents calls itself "satire." Satire is defined as a literary work that ridicules (through exaggeration and joke) human folly or vice, usually with the aim of betterment or, at least, edification. In the words of Evelyn Waugh, satire "presupposes homogeneous moral standards" on the strength of which the reader can analyze and condemn the behavior shown. That means, in literary tradition and especially in the utopian novel, the reader should finish the book with an idea of how things could be improved. *The Sentimental Agents* fails to provide this counterconcept. It denounces (rather wordily, one might add) rhetoric, revolution, and group spirit. But as an alternative it offers nothing but the catchword "Necessity" (73). While Klorathy claims to know what "the Necessity" is, he refuses to divulge its secrets, insisting that the natural course of the battle between good and evil makes this the best of all possible universes. None of the space novels to date attempts to describe Canopus's mother planet, on which the much-exalted principle of Necessity reigns. Therefore, since this concept is not defined, it remains essentially a rhetorical device. Worse, it brings to mind the vocabulary of history's many demagogues who have sold murderous ideologies by declaring them to be "destiny." Klorathy, who is as unemotional as a dictionary, personifies the absence of heated oratory, but not an alternative to it. Both he and Incent fail to fulfill their basic function in the novel as focal points for constructive criticism of the satirized behavior. Despite the novel's title, they are *not* sentimental, and the reader looking for identifiable personae might feel that a little sentiment could have done them no harm. For "necessity" alone is not sufficient motivation to keep turning the pages—it must be complemented by curiosity and the process of recognition.

The Marriages Between Zones Three, Four, and Five (Volume Two)

Shortly before his reincarnation as George Sherban in *Shikasta*, Johor reflects: "I passed many possibilities of slipping over into the other Zones, Zones Four and Five in particular, and, remembering the lively scenes I had observed or taken part in on past visits, it was a real effort to make myself move on."[16] Said other Zones are the scene of *Marriages*, the second volume of *Canopus in Argos*. If the phantasmal documentation presented in the other installments often makes arduous reading, this volume fairly beguiles the reader, creating a medieval, half-magical realm which can be counted among Doris Lessing's finest and most artful creations. It is safe to say that if *Marriages*, which is acclaimed by followers of both "the old" and "the new" Lessing, were the rule instead of the exception in *Canopus*, this novel sequence would be on the whole better loved.

The book's topography is depicted in chart 3. Lessing's universe consists not only of empires, galaxies and planets, but also of Zones. If we count Rohanda, these amount to the magical number of mysticism, seven.

Zones One through Six are arranged concentrically around Rohanda. Zone Six, is, like Dante's Inferno, "not for the easily swayed to pity, not for the easily horri-

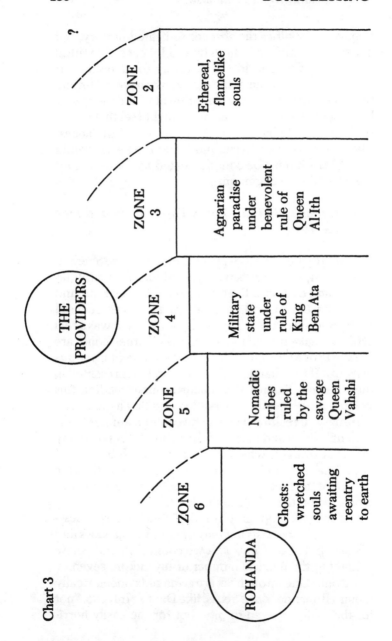

Chart 3

ZONE 2 — Ethereal, flamelike souls

ZONE 3 — Agrarian paradise under benevolent rule of Queen Al·Ith

THE PROVIDERS

ZONE 4 — Military state under rule of King Ben Ata

ZONE 5 — Nomadic tribes ruled by the savage Queen Vahshi

ZONE 6 — Ghosts: wretched souls awaiting reentry to earth

ROHANDA

fied."[17] It harbors the wretched souls who clamor for
reentry into earthly life. Next comes Zone Five, sketched
briefly in *Marriages*, inhabited by about fifty tribes, all
terrorized by the Queen's Hun-like armies, which loot
the land. Zone Four, under the rule of Ben Ata, is a lame
military state—it could prosper if not all its wealth were
poured into wars and war games. Zone Three is ruled
by the comely Queen Al·Ith: there, flora, fauna, and
human beings dwell in primeval harmony, their democratic agrarian state devoid of conflict and discord.
Above them is Zone Two, sketched again only briefly
toward the book's conclusion: its inhabitants are blue
flames, invisible to the mortal eye. They are beings "like
fire, like light . . . high and fine" (230).[18] What lies
beyond Zone Two the reader can, so far, only surmise.

Though concentrically organized around the Ro-
handan center, the zones are geographically connected.
From Zone Four, one can reach the capital of Zone
Three, Andaroun, in a few days on horseback. But
travel between the Zones is, until the events of *Marriages*, infrequent, since the Zone-dwellers do not think
beyond their given frontiers. They despise and vaguely
fear the terrains lower (thus more barbaric) than their
own, and are discouraged from looking upward to the
higher regions, where the air is ever more rarefied, the
quality of life quicker and more abstract.

The Providers who rule over all Zones decree that
Zone Three's wise Queen Al·Ith shall go to Zone Four to
marry its King, Ben Ata. The morganatic marriage takes
place and the couple, who at first perceive each other as
utterly, irrevocably foreign, gradually develop a deep
spiritual and physical affinity. This union is celebrated
by a celestial drum which beats day and night; their son
Arusi is born, a child meant to fuse "the imaginations of
two realms." But when he is half a year old, the drum-
beat ceases and the Providers order Al·Ith to return to
her old Zone. Ben Ata is to marry the heathen Queen of

Zone Five, a female Genghis Khan named Vahshi. Al·Ith returns to Zone Three, but her own people, now ruled by her sister Murti', ostracize her. She drifts from Andaroun to the borders of Zone Two, where she mourns for her husband and child in bitter exile (in fact one of Lessing's most heartrending episodes). Spiritually, she has already departed from Zone Three to the higher realm, into which she one day disappears.

To interpret the book as a diagnosis of the "ancient battle between men and women" (jacket copy) would be to focus on only one aspect, and not even a crucial one. *Marriages* depicts, rather, the battle between the familiar and the foreign, the struggle to go beyond domestic borders and adopt the ways of the "other," the strange and unfamiliar. The essence of strangeness is, for the heroine Al·Ith, certainly not limited to the male-female polarity in her marriage, but includes all the ways of Zone Four, from the awkward clothing, the hierarchical rituals and customs, the absurd use of force to control man and beast; to the very air, which is thick and oppressive. Al·Ith is a stranger in a strange land, forced to forsake her place in the realm she knows to be right and good, and take on the "otherness" of a nether world. She is thus a catalyst for the expansion of both Zones' perspectives—a process to which she, as an individual, falls victim.

An interpretation of the novel must take into consideration two viewpoints: that of Al·Ith, and that of the Providers. The latter (who are neither identified explicitly as "Canopus" nor defined more closely at all) give the marriage order concurrently with a sudden falling off in fertility in both Zones Three and Four. Presumably, the marriage is intended to rectify matters: the parallel but independent functioning of the Zones has gone awry, and now a gradual synthesis is necessary. Indeed, the merging of realms has the desired effect: Ben Ata is gradually transfigured by his wife's

intuitive sense of the noble and genuine in life, as well as
her intelligent command of personal and governmental
crises. She gives him her "largeness and freedom of
being" and convinces him, among other things, that his
land will never prosper until its strength is invested in
agriculture and housing rather than in war. He stream-
lines his army and initiates the slow but unmistakable
evolution of Zone Four from a martial to a social state.
Ben Ata even lifts the restrictions against gazing toward
Zone Three (previously punishable by a weighted
helmet which held the wearer's head tilted downwards). Now an enlightened ruler, Ben Ata literally
teaches his people to look upwards. When he marries
Vahshi, he passes on Al·Ith's wise modes of thought,
and even in barbaric Zone Five the seeds of democratic
government germinate. As a further result, migrations
between the Zones start to occur: the dwellers may not
only look toward higher things, figuratively speaking,
but now have the option of actual emigration to a higher
Zone. Among many others, Dabeeb, Al·Ith's friend
(and one of the author's favorite creations), eventually
migrates to Zone Three. Ben Ata comes there only once,
to visit Al·Ith at her border zone hermitage before her
departure to Zone Two. But Arusi is to be raised partly
in his mother's Zone, over which he will someday rule.

The relative backwardness of the Zones' civilization is unambiguously expressed by their relationship to
war—militant behavior is directly related to primitivity
(as opposed to Rohanda, where the arms race stands for
"progress"). As a result of Al·Ith's influence, both zones
Four and Five modify their warlike ways for the better.
But Zone Three, as well, adopts a new relationship to
war: this previously peaceable society now has a concept of armed conflict and finds it necessary to defend
its borders with medieval cudgels and catapults. Nevertheless, Zone Three's retrogression is small compared to
the progress of the realms below, and the Providers

doubtlessly see the entire situation as markedly improved.

From Al·Ith's viewpoint, things are not so simple as for the master planners. For her, an intact world order suddenly snaps out of place and becomes, with no evident reason, disorderly and irrational. Conditions in her own zone begin to falter even before the marriage decree. But unlike the world of antiquity, which could be restored to order by atonement of personal sin, Al·Ith's realm goes amiss through no fault of her own. The maladies in the queendom are completely beyond her control; understood, if at all, only by the Providers. Nevertheless, her subjects hold her responsible for the falling off of crops and livestock, their own melancholy, and even for the marriage itself, which they see as the beginning of infiltration and corruption from below. Al·Ith, a scrupulously moral and responsible queen, searches her memory for mistakes she might have made—there are none, since she has always obeyed the Providers' laws. These, it appears, have used Al·Ith to initiate flux between the two spheres and to "produce" an heir who will benefit both. Once she has served this classical dynastic function, she is pushed out of Zone Four to make room for Ben Ata's new wife and the entanglement of Zone Five in the Providers' machinations. That she, now contaminated by a lower Zone, cannot be reaccepted in her own Zone is irrelevant: she has outlived her usefulness as a catalyst and is banished to the borders for the rest of her days. Thus the real crux of the female-male question in *Marriages* is not the rivalry and ensuing poignant communion of husband and wife, but the hopeless position of the female manipulated by the patriarchal establishment, which values her only as a means to bear male progeny. It is small comfort to be assured that Al·Ith is merely being "properly and soberly prepared" (197) for her soul's return to Zone Two.

This tale is narrated by Lusik, one of Al·Ith's "mind fathers" (men who provide mental and spiritual nourishment to children, as opposed to the biological role of the "gene father"). Lusik's tone reflects a conflict present in many Canopean archivists' reports: though scrupulously concerned with accuracy, to the point of analyzing every possible bias in his own viewpoint, the chronicle nevertheless reveals deep emotional involvement with the players and events. Lusik's poetic and moving narrative utilizes insight into the protagonists' emotions that easily equals that of the traditional omniscient narrator. While admitting his sympathy for Al·Ith, he tries to preserve a "correct" picture of her which will right Zone Three's erroneous memory. To this end, he not only analyzes the many portraits of her, as varied as the renditions of the madonna with child, but also refers repeatedly to the songs and ballads, which assume an important structuring function in this book. Events are previewed, exemplified, and, later, recorded by means of song. When Al·Ith needs illumination on any subject, she seeks its reflection in the current street songs.

In a lengthy episode exactly midway in the text, she suggests that a song festival of Zone Four's women and children be organized to teach her the new customs, only to find out that the women, led by Dabeeb, already gather regularly in top security to repeat the old verses and learn new ones. This is their way of sustaining the "race memory"—a ritual from which the men are totally excluded, if they know of it at all. Later, the women claim the right of pilgrimage to Zone Three on the grounds that "it was they who had kept the old knowledge alive for so long" (219). Dabeeb is chief songmaker and consequently the sole recipient of the Providers' orders, which she communicates to Ben Ata and Al·Ith. It is important to emphasize that it is not the songs content (which is often banal) but the procedure of singing which crystallizes as all-important in *Marriages*. Songmaking ability attests to the intact spirituality of women (and children): while the men are out squandering time and money on wars, the integrity of the race is kept alive through feminine rituals. At the same time, these role patterns conform to the medieval concepts of masculine and feminine—women are granted intuitive and extrasensory powers as a consolation prize for their exclusion from weightier matters such as warring and administration.

The songs, like the Providers' orders, are of unknown origin. Though they can usually be traced to one Zone or the other, no one knows who first learned them—they seem to emerge from a collective subconscious. All the more odd that they, again in analogy to the orders, are universally accepted as truth. This brings us to the book's most problematical point: the question of obedience and free will. The Zone dwellers, obeying as they do mandates coming from "above" without questioning their source, are on a pre-enlightenment level, easily comparable to citizens in the Middle Ages who believed in devils and witches that they had never seen. Further, Lessing fails to throw critical light on this obedience. The Zone subjects are not depicted as ignorant but rather as enjoying harmony with a universal master plan, referred to here again as "the Necessity" (121). It has never occurred to anyone in more than a fleeting way to even wonder who the Providers are—least of all Al·Ith, who is deprived of the very basis of her existence at their whim. Only Dabeeb's husband, Jarnti, now an old soldier at loose ends since there are no more wars to fight, dares to assert: "Dabeeb, you talk of the Providers ... one'd think you knew them the way you talk! But they take everything away." To which Dabeeb gives the docile reply, "We have to believe they know what they are doing, my dear" (236). This religious, medieval resignation to the will of the higher-ups cannot help but rankle in the reader's mind. It is out of place in the twentieth century, rendered more than obsolete by historical examples demonstrating the dangers of the Führer principle. Characters cannot be seriously motivated by the argument that they are "just following orders." Thus, while *Marriages* is an enticing book with many passages of timeless relevance, the serflike mentality of its Zone dwellers makes them, for the reader, a hairbreadth less than believably human.

Nonetheless, the text lends itself well to a broad range of interpretive approaches. Irony has it that with *Marriages*, the author—who outspokenly criticizes and rejects Christianity[19]—has been credited with writing a Christ-parable, Al·Ith being the female savior who descends to a baser realm, sows the seeds of redemption and is then agonizingly reunited with her true spiritual home.[20] The book could as easily be interpreted along the lines of the platonic image of the cave. It shows people who consider what they observe in their own limited Zones to be "real." Those who are able, however, to emerge from the cavelike confines into a lighter realm, as Al·Ith dissolves into the blue flames of Zone Two or Dabeeb seeks the rarefied air of Zone Three, realize that they have been accustomed to a flickering, pitifully dim reflection of reality: "The point is, we are all so used to it, we no longer see how bad it is."[21] The expansion of perspective by the crossing of boundaries, then, is *Marriages'* transcendent theme: it is limited only by the fact that the search for new vision has to be ordered from above.

It is not possible at this point to reach final conclusions about the *Canopus* novels, since at least one volume is still forthcoming. There is absolutely no question, however, that with them a new phase in the reception and evaluation of Lessing's work has begun. Disgruntled readers complain that large portions of the

new books are "bleak, painful to read and stiffly written" but must admit that they are "bound to have their
special fans."[22] Though they deviate radically from the
more palatable fiction of Lessing's earlier years, they
are definitely representative for certain current trends.
They appear at a time when ever larger portions of
Western populations believe in different forms of life
on other planets. At this writing, a creature called
"E.T." has virtually become a national obsession in
America. On an official, but hardly less amusing, plane,
many scientists have called for "a global effort to listen
for radio signals from any extraterrestrials who may be
living on planets of other stars,"[23] while *vox populi*
accuses government of devious cover-ups regarding
UFOs. No doubt, the space novels fall on fertile
ground, especially with young readers. For the older
reader familiar with the development of Lessing's
ideas, it is clear that her point lies not in the truth or
falsehood of the fantasies, but in their potential to provoke change in "how people see themselves."[24]

   Canopus in Argos delivers a black prognosis for
human rights and freedoms as we know them, yet the
books doggedly assert that life will not only go on but
will be transmuted to a finer and better stage. The
future holocaust will be survived by a handful who will
rise like the Phoenix from the ashes to reestablish touch
with life's very essence; the reader is led through a
labyrinth of senseless misery only to hear at the end that
it all has been to a higher purpose. This transcendental
optimism has been decried as the books' weakest fea-
ture, a false Brave New World sentimentality which
frustrates rather than convinces. One could apply to
Lessing a criticism made of Gustav Mahler's music—it
is at its shallowest when affirmative and optimistic. The
reader, according to individual disposition, may see
Lessing's new optimism as an insult to intelligence, or as
a deus ex machina solution to otherwise insoluble con-

flicts. Undoubtedly, it testifies to the author's tenacious faith in the human race. When asked to justify her conception of a world where cosmic "necessity" weighs heavier than suffering and free will, she uses words like "optimism," "faith," or "survival." Her current perspective, it seems, is determined not by reason and logic, but by hope and her belief in the human race's talent for self-preservation: "the world is full of babies. Well, I like to think some of them will survive, perhaps even better."[25]

8

Journalism, *Zeitgeist* and Autobiography: Nonfiction

"The only thing that really matters in life is not wealth or poverty, pleasure or hardship, but the nature of the human beings with whom one is thrown into contact, and one's relation with them."[1] This maxim from Lessing's essay on Olive Schreiner could serve as a motto for her nonfictional works, which always pursue the human center of the given topic. Both essays and fictional writings have in common the author's engaging eloquence and keen eye for "the quintessential eccentricity of the human race."[2] Thus, the nonfictional texts should be recommended reading for all enthusiasts of Lessing's novels. Available to the general reader in book form are an autobiographical reportage on Africa (*Going Home*, 1957), two lengthy essays which cross into the terrain of novel and short story (*In Pursuit of the English*, 1960; and *Particularly Cats*, 1967), and the interviews, essays, and critiques collected in *A Small Personal Voice* (1975) under the editorship of Paul Schlueter. Though this anthology contains only a smattering of Lessing's sundry nonfictional works, it is a gem among her books and should not only hold a central place in any study of her thinking but also fairly cries out to be followed up by a sequel.

The essay is by nature one step closer to its author than is fiction. It deals in the dynamic development of opinions rather than in plots and images. And because the author's viewpoint changes continually, readers must be wary of attaching absolute significance to any essayistic statement: witness Lessing's 1957 eulogy on realism as the "highest form" of prose, in contrast to her recent view that it is dead or at best irrelevant.[3] As Lessing puts it, "Writers suffer a unique fate: it is taken for granted that what [other] people say when they are twenty, or thirty, or for that matter forty or fifty, is not what they will be saying later. But a writer's most ill-considered thought, most immature remark, will be quoted back at her, him, for ever."[4] Essays and interviews should not be seen as monuments to a finite idea but as a long chain of building blocks in the idea's development.

The lighter side of Lessing's nonfiction is best illustrated by the two volumes *In Pursuit of the English* and *Particularly Cats.* The latter is not well-known, probably for the reason that in a world which seems to fall into clear-cut fronts of cat-lovers and cat-haters, the reader must share its interest in the topic in order to read it at all. Cats, credited with supernatural wisdom since the beginnings of civilization, have a traditional place in literature as silent observers of human folly. They are the standard companions of sorcerers, seers, eccentrics, and kooks of all sorts. Mummified with supreme honors in ancient Egypt, burned alive in medieval attempts to exorcise devils, their status has ranged from highest esteem to blackest disfavor. Lessing describes felines with an almost classical mixture of attraction and repulsion, though the former overrides. Her reminiscences reach all the way back to her early childhood in Persia. The book's central episode—nothing less than a full-scale cat holocaust—takes place on the African farm, but most of its anecdotes are devoted to Lessing's two London house cats, "grey cat" and "black cat." Grey cat is arrogant, willful and shamefully lacking in maternal instinct; black cat, in contrast, is a humble and devoted mother. Needless to say, grey cat, the tyrannical matron, is tormented by jealous hatred of her sensual, earthy housemate, whom she would gladly rip to pieces. The two grimalkins' armed truce just barely overrides their instinctive animosity—only the moral pressure from their disapproving mistress keeps them from going at each other's throats.

Lessing's interest in cats is no doubt inspired by this paradox of decorum and instinct. The house cat is an animal that always wavers between civilization and nature. Its domestication is tentative, and the ties to its savage ancestors strong. In Africa, these bonds are ever present in the form of the nearby veld, which tantalizes all erring felines. Many cats "go wild," abandon the niceties of domestic behavior, and return to primeval existence. Going wild is almost equally tempting for some canines ("The Story of Two Dogs"), and occasionally even for human beings ("The Story of a Non-Marrying Man"). Lessing emphasizes that the rituals of domestication are for cats—as for children—but a thin veneer covering a secret, sibylline world: "the cats were not conscious of humans. They were relating to each other only, like children in rivalry, for whom adults are manoeuvreable, bribable objects, outside the obsession. . . . "[5]

Thus for the city dweller surrounded by buildings, machines, and pavements, cats embody a relatively intact natural microcosm. As overseer of this microcosm, the cat-enthusiast must make the decisions to destroy or save life, to enable or prevent birth. Matings, pregnancies, births, and illnesses are to be regarded as *Particularly Cats'* major events; the balance of life and death its main theme. Though nature appears to be imperfect, offering too many kittens too soon and too often, the essayist astutely observes that the birthrate was correct for primeval conditions (under which only one or two kittens of a litter would survive). Mother nature stubbornly refuses to adjust the cat-production (like the sexual drive and the hunting instinct) to civilization, and the serious threat of rampant overpopulation forces human beings to become "murderers"—so Lessing's description of herself and her father after a raid with a mini-gas-chamber filled with chloroform, to rid the farm from virtual armies of cats. The impartial reader might argue that the modern cat-keeper lives up to the traditional image of oddball when he or she refuses to spay a cat, considering this a more callous infraction on nature's autonomy than the eventual and inevitable drowning of kittens.

Lessing's essayistic reflections on cats provide a stepping-stone for her ever deeper and subtler assessment of the species. History has demonstrated often enough that humans can behave like animals. Lessing turns the tables and infuses her animals with a respectable repertoire of human emotion—fury, vindictiveness, spite, hurt feelings, pride, mourning, triumph. There seems to be something all too human about a cat's rapt and selfish devotion to its own neuroses. As one of the London cats' many fascinated observers remarks in anguish: " 'Look at it,' said she, 'that's us. That's what we're like.' " As previously mentioned, Lessing's novels after 1969 will consistently emphasize the loftier sensibilities of the dumb beast, an aspect epitomized in the cat-dog Hugo of *Memoirs.*

Particularly Cats remains a beguiling book, though it does not aspire to depth or import. Through the felines' complex interaction, expressed in "signals of a different kind, which we are too crude to catch," it calls the reader's attention to the inner logic of nature's laws. Though these can be demonstrated as well by plants (as in *Briefing*) or by greylag geese, for that matter, it is particularly cats, whose primeval instincts thrive in the thick of the metropolis, but whose neurotic reaction to

civilization is so singularly human, who often uphold
the city dweller's touch with nature.

In Pursuit of the English is like the treatise on
felines in that it describes a secret, closed order which
outsiders can observe and, according to their disposition, hate or admire, but never really enter. The book-
length essay describes Lessing's experiences during her
first year in London (1949-1950), and testifies to the
proximity of fiction and documentary. It reads much
like a novel, and only on the last page (when the narrator is referred to as "Doris") are we reminded of its
autobiographical nature. In its current American edition, the book is a victim of dime-romance marketing.
The cover allures the prospective buyer with promises
of a "spellbinding saga" involving a "web of drama and
passion," and an "unforgettable revelation of the naked
heart"(!).[6] In fact, it is a witty and well-tempered satire
on the trials of apartment hunting in postwar London—
a task made interesting, if not easier, by the hovering
"agents" eager to con the homeless out of their earnest-
money. The book is unique among Lessing's work in
that it consistently approaches its characters from a
humorous angle, grinning tolerantly at their individual
quirks and rituals (which range from infuriating to outright exploitative). Lessing's ire against parochialism
and narrow-mindedness is left aside for the course of
this one text. The English, like the family of felines,
provide the "easy listening" category of her repertoire—and the essay is a must for devotees of her prose.

The book opens in Africa, describing Lessing's ear-
liest contact with British settlers, of whom her father
was one, but quickly moves to London. Its main setting
is the boardinghouse run by Flo and Dan, a completely
unintelligent but shrewd couple who are in to make a
killing on the postwar housing shortage. The lovingly
drawn main figure is Rose, whom the reader will recognize from the short story "The Other Woman," an

underpaid shopgirl who attracts potential tenants like
the narrator to the house. Rose is opinionated, persnick-
ety, and prudish, but eminently likable; she stands firm
on her principles, no matter how irrational they may be.
She is a master in the art of creating a meaningful
microcosm within a megalopolis: Within gigantic London, Rose has created an intangible "tunnel" of familiarity only a few blocks long, from which she seldom
strays. Not that she has ever pursued life in the big
city—as the narrator tries to do—she does not have the
faintest idea how big it is, nor does she care to find out.
Her goals are simple (marriage, motherhood, and a
house of her own), her interests clear-cut (the price of
nail polish, her boyfriend). Her world is ruled by an
inner logic which has no connection to reality. While
bitterly resenting the peacetime social state, she pines
for the recent war which, with high wages and patriotic
fervor, made her happy. During the war, "people liked
each other. Well, they don't now, do they? And so don't
talk to me about your socialism, it just makes me sick
and tired, and that's the truth" (122). Rose has a natural
talent for getting to the heart of matters. When Dan and
Flo go to court to evict the house's original prewar
owners, Rose alone can boil down the high-flown legal
jargon and recognize the brutal pragmatism underlying
it: "All they want you to do is tell a good lie and stick to it
afterwards" (180). Rose exemplifies the simple person's
dream of a simple life, with old-fashioned morals and
unambiguous concepts of proper behavior. The sadly
intolerant side of her righteousness is demonstrated
when she ends her friendship with the narrator—who
commits the heinous crime of being polite to a prostitute.

Dan and Flo, for all of Lessing's attempts to illuminate their comical sides, are not particularly funny. Any
reader who has dealt with nasty landlords will be left
with a familiar bad taste by this couple. Dan is a sub-
verbal animal who communicates by teeth-gnashing
rather than speech. He is violent with his tenants, beats

his children, and makes his money off shady housing deals. Flo is the up-and-coming landlady who thinks of little but sex and money; other people are to her nothing more than potential rent payers. The narrator is finally driven from the house by their greed, since they are determined to rent her rooms more profitably. London around 1950 thus seems to teem with profiteers and schemers, among them Bobby Brent (alias MacNamara and Ponsonby), a roving swindler or "spiv" who stays on the narrator's heels from start to finish. He is a compulsive wheeler-dealer who cons people on principle, even when he has nothing to gain from it.

As the title indicates, the narrator starts out in pursuit—literally, since she sails halfway around the world to come to her parents' homeland; and figuratively, as she seeks the elusive passwords for dealing with the British mentality. If a clear statement can be made about the British subjects shown here, it is that their irrationality and stubbornness is unsurpassed. Dan, Flo, and Bobby Brent represent the "nation of shopkeepers" (Disraeli); their need to exploit is the first commandment. The do's and don'ts of English protocol escape simple logical analysis: as an anecdote in *Going Home* illustrates, it is the Anglo-Saxons who can treat like dogs people *born* with a darker skin color, but who spend hundreds of hours roasting their own skins brown as a symbol of wealth and leisure. Their ritualized miniature world obscures the relationship between important events and trivia: to people like Rose, social and political progress is irrelevant, the price of nail polish, on the other hand, a serious matter. At the book's conclusion, the narrator has ceased expecting people to act reasonably. Wise to the pesky con-man, impervious to the wheedling landlady, she is no longer in pursuit of the English mentality, for "like love and fame it is a platonic image, a grail, a quintessence, and by definition, unattainable" (11).

A more earnest note is struck by Lessing's other

nonfiction works. *A Small Personal Voice* contains two essays on the novel, considerable biographical material, six literary reviews, and two essays on Africa. The book sheds light on many of Lessing's themes, among them communism, politics, strife between black and white, social struggle, feminism, and the ethical responsibility of literature. It particularly illuminates Lessing's relationship to communism, which was crucial to her work throughout the 1950s. She describes herself in the title essay (1957) as "a writer who has for many years been emotionally involved in the basic ethical conflict of communism—what is due to the collective and what to the individual conscience. . . . "[7] This question is and remains the mainstay of Doris Lessing's work, long after she declared her skepticism regarding both the Communist party and its literary exponents ("the cheerful little tract about economic advance"). "The Small Personal Voice" expresses Lessing's early faith in socialism and in the writer's obligation to enlighten and edify, to provoke thought and break down the barriers that block understanding between nations. The essay is a singularly persuasive appeal to authors and readers to recognize the humane goals of socialist commitment, which transcend self-interest:

> All over that enormous land mass, the Soviet Union and China, the most epic movement of change ever known in history is taking place. It is the greatest event of our time, and one in which we are all involved . . . everywhere in the world people with nothing to gain from being socialists . . . have become, are becoming, and will become, socialists of one kind or another.[8]

A second major examination of the novelist's relationship to society, reprinted here as a counterpart to the 1957 essay, is the Preface to *The Golden Notebook*,

written in 1971 for a reissue. It discusses the first decade
of the novel's reception, emphasizing that most readers
saw only isolated segments of its argumentation, or
made the mistake of turning to the "authorities" to learn
the "right" interpretation. Those who saw what the
novel was trying to do, says Lessing, were the readers
familiar with Marxism and its emphasis on the *interrelation* of facets. The two essays bespeak the inseparability of literature from social theory in Lessing's formative years.

The interviews in *A Small Personal Voice* document many of the stations in Lessing's development
during the 1960s (they date from 1963, 1966, and 1969),
especially her gradual loss of hope for a betterment of
humanity's predicament in our century. Until the Soviet invasion of Hungary in 1956, Lessing still believed
that existing Communist states might become more
democratic and that a "new man" would be born. Her
current view is radically different—she sees modern
history as a stampede toward self-destruction. Not only
have Communist countries failed to make the hoped-
for progress toward individual freedoms and human
rights; Western capitalist countries are increasingly
ruled by large-scale greed and ruthless pursuance of
their rapacious self-interest. Both factions, as Lessing
has noted repeatedly, pour funds which could feed and
clothe their entire populations into armament. During
the 1960s, the author increasingly shifted her emphasis
from the group goals of socialism to an appeal for
individual integrity, civil courage, and refusal to conform:

> I think the most valuable citizens any country can
> possess are the troublemakers, the public nuisances. . . . No government, no political party
> anywhere cares a damn about the individual. That
> is not their business. . . . So—to the barricades,

> citizens! If we don't fight every inch of the way,
> we'll find ourselves with our numbers tattooed on
> our wrists yet.[9]

While her essays unequivocally encourage dissent, the
1960s left Lessing—like thousands of other liberals—
embittered about the fate of rebels in our society. She
repeatedly warns of existing fascist regimes and related
totalitarian states, with their monumental efficiency in
squelching reform and ignoring civil rights. Conservative powers had disbanded the "Old Left" to which she
belonged and were soon to silence the New Left of the
late 1960s. The above endorsement of dissenters was
made in 1967, as the American student movement
gathered strength for its brief peak of radical agitation,
spurred by the conviction that slow, evolutionary
democratic change would never come to pass in the
American system.

Though Lessing no longer shared the youth movement's hope for revolution, she did share the insight that
polite, patient persuasion is pointless. In Africa, as she
says, "I had spent fifteen years arguing, day in, day out,
with my family and almost all the white people I knew,
about the monstrousness of the society we lived in. All
that argument had not changed anybody's mind by a
fraction."[10] This point is demonstrated repeatedly in
Lessing's anecdotes—it could almost be identified as
their unifying leitmotif. She recalls being detained in
South Africa as a teenager by an official who doggedly
insisted on classifying her as an "Asiatic," oblivious to
her white skin and British nationality: "You were born in
Persia? . . . Then you are an Asiatic." With the classic
gesture of racial discrimination, she is escorted to the
back of the train. In a later essay, Lessing quotes a Sufi
story describing a man whose own obsession leads him
to conclude that the dictionary is a book about money:
of a hundred thousand entries, he has noticed only the

handful that deal with finances. Lessing cites another
Sufi story to describe humanity's effect on the course
of history. It depicts a mouse which has a cow on a leash
and of course "cannot control the cow. But as the cow
stops to eat some grass it shouts 'that's right, eat up some
grass' and when the cow turns left it shouts 'that's right,
turn left'."[11] Lessing's is a bleak view of history—but it is
not atypical for her generation, and certainly is backed
up by historical examples. Nevertheless, even in her
latest essay to date (the Afterword to volume four of
Canopus in Argos) she emphasizes the crucial importance of an idealistic individual vision which transcends
the political realities of the day.

The necessity of dissent and validity of the outsider's standpoint are also the unifying themes of Lessing's
reviews and critiques. On topics so diverse as the early
feminist Olive Schreiner or the militant black organizer
Malcolm X, she invariably defends the right to civil
disobedience and minority action. Her discussions of
other writers (which she undertakes very selectively)
are supportive and subtle. They stop short of the political essays' strong polemical stance, and resort occasionally to the jejune understatement (such as calling Malcolm X's death "a pity"). Her sensitive portrait of the
Danish Baroness Karen Blixen (pseudonym Isak Dinesen), one of the century's most colorful literary figures,
refrains from pinpointing the critical difference between
Dinesen's perspective and her own, which lies in Dinesen's lacking a sense of high-voltage racial or political
tension. (A comparative analysis of Dinesen's "Farah"
and Lessing's first novel, both of which deal with a
white woman and her servant in Africa, would find
virtually no similarities in tenor.) Doris Lessing is
decidedly not a literary critic, nor does she aspire to be,
but her critiques are always illuminating: of the book at
hand, the author behind it, and her own approach to
literature.

The final section of *A Small Personal Voice* contains two essays describing Lessing's experiences as a
Rhodesian "prohibited immigrant." The subject is
covered exhaustively in *Going Home*, the journal of her
1956 trip back to Africa. The American edition again
displays the makeup of a cheap romance novel, this
time whetting the potential reader's appetite for "shat-
tering discovery" and "explosive passion."[12] In fact,
Going Home is a cool and for the most part successful
mixture of three narrative levels: personal reminis-
cence, journalistic exposition, and guileless political
statement. As an autobiographical document, it is a
moving depiction of the author's attachment to Africa's
landscape and atmosphere. It contains a wealth of bit-
tersweet anecdotes relating the fates of white settlers
struggling to adapt to the colonial system, as well as
notes on the century's pre-1956 literature on Africa.
Going Home also sheds light on Lessing's original
attraction to communism through the analogy of class
and color: she has often stated that during the 1940s,
the local communist group was virtually the only circle
which actively opposed the mechanisms of racial discrimination, and in which she could voice her own rage.

The journalist's viewpoint vacillates between her
faith in a country "so empty we can dream . . . of cities
and a civilization more beautiful than anything that has
been seen in the world before" (11), and wrath against
the humiliating inequities enforced by the white minority regime. Lessing proceeds from a simple premise:
"Africa belongs to the Africans; the sooner they take it
back the better" (8). But the struggle of "taking it back"
is bound to be long and violent, since the color bar robs
the Africans of all basic freedoms. The whites sketched
here range from the unconcealed racist to the "useful
rebel," but any real white opposition is lacking, and the
African population has no access to the political process. Black leaders who become too audible are simply

given life sentences (the reader should remember that many are still jailed today, over twenty-five years later). South Africa's totalitarian regime, though so unsure of itself that it has to "prohibit" and incarcerate its critics, is nevertheless strong enough to survive for decades to come, as Lessing's 1956 journal predicts.

Politically, the book takes issue with both South Africa, "a Fascist paradise" and "one of the most brilliant police states in history,"[13] and with the Federation of the Rhodesias and Nyasaland, which existed between 1953 and 1964. Lessing calls its slogan "Partnership" a "bad joke," since it is intended to appease the Africans without giving them equality. Partnership is called apartheid in South Africa, and was propagated under the flag of "separate but equal" in the United States. It was no more successful than were initial attempts at equal education for black and white in America, where citizens defended the "integrity" of their white neighborhoods by welcoming bussed black schoolchildren with tomatoes and rotten eggs. "Separate" always includes an economic handicap so staggering that it defeats the black school/family/organization before it can begin to compete. The resulting vicious circle is described by an African political prisoner whom Lessing quotes: "the Africans are poor, and therefore their education is poor, and therefore they are poor" (74).

If we substitute "American Negro/Indian/Chicano" for "African" in statements such as the above, the extended relevance of *Going Home* to other political situations becomes clear. The book is much more than a product of its time.[14] Even though Lessing herself may today disagree with some of her earlier viewpoints, her essays of the 1950s retain their status as some of her most significant works. She may have washed her hands of politics, but they continue to carry a political message. They always reach beyond the specific situation to the general patterns of political exploitation and historical process. They teach repeatedly that the "public butchers of our time, from Eichmann up and down,"[15] are not unique individuals, but merely interchangeable parts in a pattern that can repeat itself endlessly. In their tenacious illumination of this pattern and its moving forces—such as nationalism, racial prejudice and religious fanaticism—Lessing's essays can well stand as a contemporary and relevant finale to any discussion of her works.

9

To Break Out of the Ordinary: Conclusion

A sweeping backward glance over Lessing's literary production of the last three-and-a-half decades reveals an overwhelming and often contradictory medley of ideas, themes, fictional techniques, and perspectives. The very heterogeneity of this oeuvre makes it a fitting illustration of its own foremost premise: that truth and substance cannot be smoothly compartmentalized and labeled, but are rather in constant flux. Lessing began her work in 1950 as a proponent of socialist commitment and nineteenth-century realism. Today she envisions a fantastic universe which has long cast its sights beyond the abortive isms of the twentieth century. Staid tradition complements experimental fervor; penetrating close-up portraits of individuals stand in contrast to a sublime cosmic panorama.

Though it would be simplistic to divide Lessing's production into phases, three milestones provide distinct orientation points for any survey. These are, first, the publication of *The Golden Notebook* in 1962; second, the break with realism after *The Four-Gated City* in 1969; and third, the step into space fiction after 1979. Lessing's works up to 1962 reflect the formation of her thinking through Marxist theory and her idealistic hope, as she recently joked, "that something like ten years after World War II, the world would be communist and perfect."[1] After 1962, she discarded the Kantian postulate that humanity as a whole will eventually accomplish its own enlightenment. Collective action (in the form of political groups, sex roles, institutions) increasingly became the target of her polemics, and her works concentrated on the possible expansion and evolution of the individual consciousness. After *The Four-Gated City*, the individual's quest for better, truer vision becomes progressively more detached from the problems of "reality," and Lessing's fiction concurrently turns its back on realism. Between 1971 and 1974 her novels delve in the mad, the subconscious, and the mystical spheres as wellsprings of perception. In 1979 then, the author completely trades off the real for the irreal, and invents a cosmos where virtually anything is possible in the battle between good and evil.

Scholarly research on Lessing's work is well established. Since the 1960s she has been a cause célèbre in the literary forum. Whereas noticeable reticence characterizes the reception of her later works beginning with *Briefing*, critics return again and again to the realist novels and stories of the 1950s and 1960s. Many dozens of articles and essays have been devoted to this field, ranging in quality from the vapid shoulder-patting of literary criticism's patriarchs to some of the finest analyses published today. The perusal of primary and secondary sources has been greatly facilitated by a book-length annotated bibliography published in 1981,[2] which, however, covers Lessing's work only through *Memoirs* (1974) and is badly hampered by inaccuracies and typographical errors. Nevertheless, as a compilation of the virtual deluge of studies on the author to date, it is an indispensable tool for the scholar and the student alike. Some of the secondary books on Lessing, which vary enormously in competency and scope, should also be mentioned here. All testify in their own right to the many developments in critical methods in the last two decades. The first major monograph, now long outdated but still available in most libraries, was Dorothy Brewster's *Doris Lessing*, which appeared early in Lessing's career.[3] Brewster's study covers the works through *Landlocked*—at that time in the galley-proof stage—and is typical for the apolitical, homey condescension meted out by many critics in the early 1960s. Free speculation on the feelings, likes, and dislikes of the author, as well as a good dose of personal bias contribute to some hair-raising conclusions. This volume also well demonstrates the tendency of Lessing's critics to unwittingly borrow her phraseology—up to the point of lifting whole sentences from her writings.[4]

Brewster's book was followed by Paul Schlueter's *The Novels of Doris Lessing*,[5] which presents the novels up to 1971 (*Briefing* and *Retreat to Innocence* appear as also-rans in a short final chapter). Schlueter's useful, meticulously documented reference work has as its main virtue patient and exhaustive textual analyses. Drawbacks are the too-lengthy quotations and overly reticent conclusions. Today's feminist reader will also take umbrage at certain quirks in the male point of view,[6] but on the whole, the book deserves full recognition as a ground-breaking achievement. Many subsequent monographs have been devoted to individual aspects, such as *Children of Violence*'s tree motif,[7] the dialectics of civilization and nature,[8] or the significance of the African locale.[9] These can be highly recommended to all more specialized readers. A broad-scale, extremely well-written scholarly study of the novels through *Memoirs* is Roberta Rubenstein's *The Novelistic Vision of Doris Lessing*.[10] Excellent individual interpretations, diverse information on Sufism, Jungian psychiatry, and other topics can be found here. For the student, the book's potential disadvantage lies in a scholarly focus which precludes its use as a general introduction. Since this and all other book-length studies on Lessing to date concentrate on selected novels, a gap in this field of research has been a full-scale presentation of her work in *all* genres.

Readers will find a well-rounded selection of essays and scholarly articles in the three major anthologies to date, one of which documents the 1971 MLA Lessing-session.[11] An excellent collection of articles edited by Annis Pratt and L. S. Dembo in 1974 is unfortunately out of print, but available on microfilm and also in its original form as a special issue of *Contemporary Literature*.[12] Most recently anthologized are the eight essays by British feminist scholars in *Notebooks/ Memoirs/Archives*, edited by Jenny Taylor.[13] This collection is representative in many respects of the sins and virtues of Lessing scholarship. The lion's share of attention is given to the early works—African fiction, *Children of Violence*, *The Golden Notebook*—works whose political nature makes them indispensable to the critic investigating the socio-historical and political determiners of Lessing's thought. Less convincing, however, is the volume's insistent overemphasis on the feminist question. The given inductive approach to the texts from the viewpoint of femaleness and women's literature pays dues, in this particular case, more to the critic's inclination than to the author's. Similarly, many articles adopt an overly personal and emotional standpoint which interferes with the reader/text relationship.[14] If Lessing scholarship wants to be taken seriously, gushing confessions of infatuated readers must be replaced by exacting textual analyses, especially of the more recent works. The greatest challenge to scholars in the field in the coming decade, as I see it, will be to resist the temptation to stagnate at the point of *The Golden Notebook* and make an honest attempt to negotiate the hairpin curves of Lessing's post-1970 development.

To generalize or to draw subtotals regarding an author as unpredictable and prolific as Lessing is risky.

If we search for a common denominator in her work to
date, it must lie in her insistence that there *is* an alternative way of viewing life—politics, sexuality, culture,
sanity—a new vista open to anyone willing to take off
the blinders of collectivism and seek it. This idea is
supported thematically by the child, the new generation on whom everything depends, and who epitomizes
the possibility of a better future. The search for something finer unites protagonists as diverse as Martha
Quest, who finds another geographic and psychic country, and Charles Watkins, who manages at least temporarily to drift through sea space. The Survivor is able
to step through the wall, and Planet 8's Representative
transcends the elements to achieve another form of
being. Completely apart from the contextual plausibil-
ity of these figures' faces, they convey a common message responsible for the magnetic, regenerative effect
of Lessing's books on her readers: that human beings
are not trapped, boxed, and filed inside immutable
boundaries. But this hopeful keynote also contains a
challenge. Before individuals can find a new sphere and
breed something better than themselves, they must
wake from their daily drowse in front of the TV set,
question the authority of the group mind and ultimately
find the courage to swim against the collective stream.
Lessing chides those who resign themselves to their
own limitations, for "this need to break out of our
ordinary possibilities—the cage we live in that is made
of our habits, upbringing, circumstances, and which
shows itself so small and tight and tyrannical when we
do try to break out—this need may well be the deepest
one we have."[15]

Notes

1. This Business of Being an Exile: Doris Lessing's Life and Works

1. Nissa Torrents, "Doris Lessing: Testimony to Mysticism," originally published in *La Calle* 106(1 April 1980): 42-44. Quoted here from the translation in *Doris Lessing Newsletter* 4(2/1980): 1, 12f., here p. 1.
2. There is to date no thorough biography of Lessing, partially due to her own wishes. The major autobiographical sources are *Going Home* and the essays and interviews in *A Small Personal Voice*. Some biographical information in major studies of her works is contradictory or inaccurate. A lengthy entry can be found in *Current Biography*, 1976, pp. 230-233.
3. Lessing, "My Father," in *A Small Personal Voice*, ed. Paul Schlueter (New York: Vintage, 1975), pp. 83-93, here p. 86.
4. Lessing, Introduction to *The Golden Notebook* (New York: Bantam, 1973), p. xv.
5. Lessing, *Going Home* (New York: Popular Library, 1968), p. 31.
6. Ibid., p. 43f.
7. Ibid., p. 44f.
8. Ibid., p. 30.
9. Ibid.
10. Letter from Doris Lessing to Mona Knapp dated 12 June 1982.
11. Interview with Lessing by Roy Newquist in *A Small Personal Voice* (note 3), pp. 45-60, here p. 46.
12. Thomas Wiseman, "Mrs. Lessing's Kind of Life," in *Time and Tide* 43(12 April 1962), p. 26.
13. Lessing, Introduction to *The Golden Notebook* (note 4), p. xiv.

14. Interview with Lessing by Christopher Bigsby in *The Radical Imagination and the Liberal Tradition. Interviews with English and American Novelists*, ed. Heide Ziegler and Christopher Bigsby (London: Junction, 1981), pp. 188-208, here p. 194.
15. Interview with Lessing by Jonah Raskin, in *A Small Personal Voice* (note 3), pp. 61-76, here p. 71.
16. Lessing denies this. See Dee Seligman, "The Sufi Quest," *World Literature Written in English* 12(1973): 190-206, or Nancy Shields Hardin, "The Sufi Teaching Story and Doris Lessing," *Twentieth Century Literature* 23(1977): 314-325.
17. Lessing's essay on Sufism, "In the World, Not of It," in *A Small Personal Voice* (note 3), pp. 129-137, here p. 133.
18. Letter from Doris Lessing (note 10).
19. See Bert Kaplan, ed., *The Inner World of Mental Illness* (New York: Harper and Row, 1964).
20. Interview with Lessing by Jonah Raskin (note 15), p. 72f.
21. See *Going Home* (note 5), pp. 50-52.
22. Interview by Jonah Raskin (note 15), p. 73f.
23. Interview with Nissa Torrents (note 1), p. 13.
24. Letter from Doris Lessing (note 10).
25. Interview with Jonah Raskin (note 15), p. 67.
26. When I inquired at a large local parochial bookstore why none of Lessing's titles were available there, I was informed that its policy was to stock only books whose content is "decent."
27. As formulated by H. Ichikawa in *Doris Lessing Newsletter* 1(Fall/1977): 1ff.
28. Introduction to *The Golden Notebook* (note 4), p. xviif.

2. A Splendid Backdrop to a Disgraceful Scene: African Fiction 1950-1965

1. Lessing, "My First Book," *Author* 91(1980): 11-14, here p. 11.
2. Ibid., p. 13.
3. All page numbers in parentheses in my discussion of this

novel refer to the Plume Books Edition (New York: New American Library, 1976).

4. Mary Ann Singleton, *The City and the Veld. The Fiction of Doris Lessing* (Lewisburg: Bucknell University Press, 1977), p. 82.

5. Ibid. Singleton makes this conflict both title and major premise of a valuable and well-documented study.

6. See Carol Hymowitz and Michaele Weissman, *A History of Women in America* (New York: Bantam, 1978).

7. Cf. the excellent interpretation of Moses as a "shadow" of Mary's personality by Roberta Rubenstein, *The Novelistic Vision of Doris Lessing* (Urbana: University of Illinois Press, 1979), p. 21ff.

8. For a discussion of the novel's servant motif in the greater context of African literature see Martin Tucker, *Africa in Modern Literature* (New York: Ungar, 1967), pp. 175-183.

9. Eliot's five-part poem cycle was published in 1922; on its relevance to the novel see Michael Thorpe, "The Grass is Singing," *Literary Half-Yearly* 19(1978): 17-27.

10. The book's epigraph.

11. Cf. Michael Thorpe, *Doris Lessing's Africa* (London: Evans Brothers, 1978).

12. Quote from "The Story of Two Dogs." Page numbers for these stories refer to *African Stories* (New York: Fawcett Popular Library, 1965).

13. Lessing, Introduction to *The Golden Notebook* (New York: Bantam, 1973), p. xiii.

14. Lessing, Author's Notes to *The Four-Gated City* (New York: Bantam, 1970), p. 655.

15. See especially Ellen Cronan Rose, *The Tree Outside the Window: Doris Lessing's* Children of Violence (Hanover, N.H.: University Press of New England, 1976).

16. Rubenstein (note 7), p. 65.

17. *Children of Violence* quotations after the four-volume Plume edition (New York: New American Library, 1970).

18. See Ann Barr Snitow, "The Front Line: Notes on Sex in Novels by Women, 1969-1979," in *Women. Sex and Sexuality*, ed. Catharine R. Stimpson and Ethel Spector Person (Chicago: University of Chicago Press, 1980), pp. 158-174. Further: Elaine Showalter, *A Literature of Their*

Own. British Women Novelists from Brontë to Lessing
(Princeton: Princeton University Press, 1977), pp. 298-319.

19. See Casey Miller and Kate Swift, *Words and Women*
(Garden City: Doubleday, 1976), pp. 112 and 136.

20. For an analysis of the political situation see Paul
Schlueter, *The Novels of Doris Lessing* (Carbondale:
Southern Illinois University Press, 1973), p. 46ff.

21. Ibid., p. 41.

22. Lessing in the title essay of *A Small Personal Voice*, ed.
Paul Schlueter (New York: Vintage, 1975), pp. 3-21, here
p. 14.

3. To Breed Something Better Than Ourselves: British Novels 1956-1962, Plays and Poems

1. Letter from Doris Lessing to Mona Knapp dated 12 June
1982. See also Paul Schlueter, *The Novels of Doris Lessing*
(Carbondale: Southern Illinois University Press, 1973),
p. 137.

2. Cover text of the 1959 edition of *Retreat to Innocence*
(New York: Prometheus, 1959). Page numbers in the following discussion of the book refer to this edition.

3. Dorothy Brewster, *Doris Lessing* (New York: Twayne,
1965), p. 103.

4. David Smith, *Socialist Propaganda in the Twentieth
Century British Novel* (New York: Macmillan, 1978),
p. 150.

5. All page numbers in the following discussion of the novel
refer to the standard paperback edition (New York:
Bantam, 1973).

6. See the excellent article by Anne M. Mulkeen, "Twentieth-Century Realism: The 'Grid' Structure of *The
Golden Notebook*," *Studies in the Novel* 4(1972): 262-274.

7. Cf. p. 635f.: "It's a small painful sort of courage which
is at the root of every life, because injustice and cruelty is
at the root of life. And the reason why I have only given
my attention to the heroic or the beautiful or the intelligent is because I won't accept that injustice and the

cruelty, and so won't accept the small endurance that is bigger than anything." This passage provides a good example of the slapdash style often criticized in Lessing's prose. It not only combines a plural subject with a singular verb, but hinges on the almost classic misconstruction "the reason is because."

8. Lessing's 1971 Introduction to the novel, p. ix.
9. See Alice Kahl Ladas, Beverly Whipple, and John D. Perry, *The G Spot* (New York: Holt, Rinehart and Winston, 1982).
10. See Roberta Rubenstein, "Briefing on Inner Space: Doris Lessing and R. D. Laing," *Psychoanalytic Review* 63 (Spring 1976): 83-93, and Marion Vlastos, "Doris Lessing and R. D. Laing: Psychopolitics and Prophecy," *PMLA* 91(1976): 245-258 for further explication of this idea.
11. Lessing, title essay of *A Small Personal Voice*, ed. Paul Schlueter (New York: Vintage, 1975), pp. 3-21, here p. 11.
12. The scene is prefigured much earlier on p. 210.
13. *A Small Personal Voice* (note 11), p. 21.
14. In *Second Playbill*, ed. Alan Durband (London: Hutchinson, 1973).
15. In *The Observer*, 9 November 1958, 16 November 1958, 23 November 1958, 30 November 1958, and 7 December 1958.
16. From the 1963 Author's Notes in Lessing, *Play With a Tiger* (London: Davis-Poynter, 1962; repr. 1972), n.p.
17. Ibid., 1972 postscript. See Agate Nesaule Krouse, "Doris Lessing's Feminist Plays," *World Literature Written in English* 15(1976): 305-322, which attempts to press the plays into a feminist mold.
18. Lessing, *Each His Own Wilderness*, in *New English Dramatists. Three Plays*, ed. E. Martin Browne (Harmondsworth: Penguin, 1959), p. 95.
19. See bibliographical entries in Dee Seligman, *Doris Lessing. An Annotated Bibliography of Criticism* (Westport, Conn.: Greenwood Press, 1981), p. 9.
20. Lessing, *Fourteen Poems* (Northwood: Scorpion Press, 1959), p. 16.
21. Lessing, *Briefing For a Descent Into Hell* (New York:

Vintage, 1981), p. 136. Emphasis in original.

22. See Lessing, *The Marriages Between Zones Three, Four, and Five* (New York: Vintage, 1981), p. 79f. A further variation on the relationship between verse and behavior appears in *The Sentimental Agents* (New York: Alfred A. Knopf, 1983), p. 162f.

4. Habits and Temptations: British Stories

1. Thus the label "British Stories" for these texts seems justified, and more accurate than the awkward division of the collected short texts into African and "other" or "non-African."

2. Cf. Lessing's Preface to *African Stories* (New York: Fawcett Popular Library, 1965), p. x.

3. Margaret Atack, "Towards a Narrative Analysis of *A Man and Two Women*," in *Notebooks/Memoirs/Archives. Reading and Rereading Doris Lessing*, ed. Jenny Taylor (Boston: Routledge & Kegan Paul, 1982), pp. 135-163, here p. 138.

4. Page numbers in parentheses in this chapter refer to Lessing, *Collected Stories*. Volume One: *To Room Nineteen*; Volume Two: *The Temptation of Jack Orkney* (London: Panther, 1979).

5. Interview with Lessing by Roy Newquist in Lessing, *A Small Personal Voice* (New York: Vintage, 1975), pp. 45-60, here p. 53.

6. Simone de Beauvoir, *The Second Sex* (New York: Alfred A. Knopf, 1964), p. xxiv.

7. See also Sharon Dean, "Marriage, Motherhood, and Lessing's 'To Room Nineteen,'" *Doris Lessing Newsletter* 5(1/1981): 1, 14.

8. Such as "Report on the Threatened City" and one of Lessing's most interesting surrealist/symbolist attempts, "How I Finally Lost My Heart."

9. Lessing's Introduction to *The Golden Notebook* (New York: Bantam, 1973), p. xiii.

5. Toward the Evolution of Consciousness:
The Four-Gated City 1969

1. Lessing, *Martha Quest* (New York: New American Library, 1970), p. 11.
2. Robert Musil, *The Man Without Qualities*, published in English in 1953 by Coward-McCann.
3. The book will be quoted in the following from the paperback edition (New York: Bantam, 1970), to which all page numbers in parentheses refer.
4. The motif is traced in detail by Ellen Cronan Rose, *The Tree Outside the Window: Doris Lessing's* Children of Violence (Hanover, N.H.: University Press of New England, 1976).
5. For an interpretation of Martha's chain of insights in the Sufi mode see Dee Seligman, "The Sufi Quest," *World Literature Written in English* 12(1973): 190-206.
6. Nancy M. Porter, "A Way of Looking at Doris Lessing," in *Female Studies VI*, ed. Nancy Hoffman, Cynthia Secor, and Adrian Tinsley (New York: Feminist Press, 1972), 123-138, here p. 138.
7. Interview with Lessing by Jonah Raskin in Lessing, *A Small Personal Voice* (New York: Vintage, 1975), pp. 61-76, here p. 65.
8. In the summer of 1997 (p. 648) Martha writes that she has been on the island fifteen years, which dates the catastrophe around 1982.
9. Pp. 2, 156, 290, and 448. The same point is made by the book's dedication, a Sufi teaching story.
10. Letter from Doris Lessing to Mona Knapp dated 12 June 1982.

6. A Parcel of Well-Born Maniacs:
Inner Space Fiction 1971-1974

1. For example, Douglass Bolling, "Structure and Theme in *Briefing For a Descent Into Hell*," in *Doris Lessing. Critical Studies*, ed. Annis Pratt and L. S. Dembo (Madison: University of Wisconsin Press, 1974), 133-147, esp. p. 135.

2. A point well made by Phyllis Chesler, *Women and Madness* (New York: Avon, 1972), and many others.

3. An extensive investigation of the book's symbols can be found in the article by Bolling (note 1).

4. Page numbers in the discussion of *Briefing* refer to Lessing, *Briefing For a Descent Into Hell* (New York: Random House, 1981).

5. It has been argued (though without much support from the text) that Watkins's recovery is merely a ploy. See Robert S. Ryf, "Beyond Ideology: Doris Lessing's Mature Vision," *Modern Fiction Studies* 21(1975): 193-201.

6. For an excellent comparison in this vein see Roberta Rubenstein, "Briefing on Inner Space: Doris Lessing and R. D. Laing," *Psychoanalytic Review* 63(1976): 83-93.

7. Lessing, *Shikasta* (New York: Vintage, 1981), p. 83.

8. See Annis Pratt, *Archetypal Patterns in Women's Fiction* (Bloomington: Indiana University Press, 1981). Page numbers in the text refer to Lessing, *The Summer Before the Dark* (New York: Bantam, 1974).

9. Quoted from Josephine Hendin, "Doris Lessing: The Phoenix 'Midst her Fires,'" *Harper* 346(June 1973): 83-86, here p. 85.

10. Ibid., p. 84.

11. Roberta Rubenstein, *The Novelistic Vision of Doris Lessing* (Urbana: University of Illinois Press, 1979), p. 212.

12. It has been suggested that the book inspired Drabble's *The Middle Ground*: see Ellen Cronan Rose, "Twenty Questions," *Doris Lessing Newsletter* 4(2/1980): 5.

13. Rubenstein (note 11), p. 240.

14. Page numbers in the discussion of *Memoirs* refer to Lessing, *The Memoirs of a Survivor* (New York: Bantam, 1976).

15. Betsy Draine, "Changing Frames: Doris Lessing's *Memoirs of a Survivor*," *Studies in the Novel* 11(1979): 51-62, here p. 56.

16. Ibid.

17. Cf. p. 156f. Feminist critics have remarked repeatedly that Lessing's rare references to lesbianism always imply it to be degenerate.

18. This stands on a different sheet altogether, of course, from the novel's deliberately nonsexist language. Lessing uses such pronoun constructions as "if a man or woman ... he, she" (p. 209) or "a person ... she" (p. 127), a welcome change from the eternal person/he of English prose.

7. This is a Catastrophic Universe: *Canopus in Argos.* Outer Space Fiction 1979-1983

1. Canopus is in fact a Giant Star with luminosity two thousand times that of the sun, about one hundred light-years distant. It is the brightest star of the constellation Carina and the second brightest in the sky. Argos, on the other hand, is a city in Greece of very ancient origins. Title quote taken from the first page of *Shikasta.*
2. Strictly speaking, the *Canopus* novels can most accurately be called "space fiction" or utopian novels rather than science fiction, which deals with the effect of *actual science* on human beings. Mystical elements such as reincarnations and telepathy go beyond the boundaries of the scientifically possible.
3. Interview with Lessing by Jonah Raskin in Lessing, *A Small Personal Voice* (New York: Vintage, 1975), pp. 61-76, here p. 70.
4. Interview by Lesley Hazleton, "Doris Lessing on Feminism, Communism and 'Space Fiction,' " *New York Times Magazine* 131(25 July 1982), p. 20ff.
5. Personal note from Doris Lessing to Mona Knapp dated 5 April 1983.
6. Page numbers in parentheses in the discussion of *Shikasta* refer to the paperback edition Lessing, *Re: Colonised Planet 5. Shikasta* (New York: Vintage, 1981).
7. Lessing's Preface to the book, quoted in the following discussion after Lessing, *The Sirian Experiments* (New York: Vintage, 1982).
8. Review of the novel by Roberta Rubenstein in *Doris Lessing Newsletter* 5(1/1981): 9f., here p. 10.
9. Cf. Lessing's Afterword to *The Making of the Represen-*

tative for Planet 8 (New York: Alfred A. Knopf, 1982), p. 123.

10. Ibid.

11. The plot of *The Making* is sketched on p. 58 of *The Sirian Experiments*. Similarly, Ambien's letter to Klorathy (p. 284f.) already appeared in *Shikasta* (p. 265). Cross-references like these are too thinly strewn, however, to really interconnect the books.

12. Interview by Hazleton (note 4). Lessing remarks on ice ages: "Compared to *that* threat, nuclear war is a puppy."

13. *The Sirian Experiments* (note 7), p. 218.

14. Volyn is a region of the USSR—it is possible that Lessing deliberately implicates the rhetorical devices of communism which she now repudiates. Volans, on the other hand, is a small constellation in the southern skies with no major stars. The book is quoted in the following after the first edition (New York: Alfred A. Knopf, 1983).

15. English translation published in New York (Orgone Institute Press) 1946; originally *Massenpsychologie des Faschismus* (1933).

16. *Shikasta* (note 6), p. 205.

17. Ibid., p. 207.

18. All page numbers refer to Lessing, *The Marriages Between Zones Three, Four, and Five (as Narrated by the Chroniclers of Zone Three)* (New York: Vintage, 1981). The words "high," "light," and "fine" also serve as the book's leitmotifs.

19. See interview with Lessing by Christopher Bigsby in *The Radical Imagination and the Liberal Tradition*, ed. Heide Ziegler and Christopher Bigsby (London: Junction, 1981), pp. 188-208, esp. p. 201; as well as *The Sentimental Agents* (note 14), p. 100f.

20. Barbara Hill Rigney, *Lilith's Daughters. Women and Religion in Contemporary Fiction* (Madison: University of Wisconsin Press, 1982), esp. p. 30ff. Rigney maintains that for Lessing, "all humanity is potentially Christlike"[!] (p. 33).

21. Lessing's Introduction to *The Golden Notebook* (New York: Bantam, 1973), p. xvii.

22. A critique of *The Making* in *Publishers Weekly* 220(18

December 1981), p. 60.

23. Quote from *Science* magazine, reported by UPI on 22 October 1982.

24. Interview with Bigsby (note 19), p. 193.

25. Ibid., p. 207.

8. Journalism, *Zeitgeist* and Autobiography: Nonfiction

1. Lessing, Afterword to Olive Schreiner, *The Story of an African Farm* (New York: Fawcett World Library, 1968; pp. 273-90), quoted here after the reprint in Lessing, *A Small Personal Voice*, ed. Paul Schlueter (New York: Vintage, 1975), pp. 97-120, here p. 120. Title quote for this chapter ibid., p. 99.

2. Lessing, *In Pursuit of the English* (New York: Popular Library, 1960), p. 5.

3. See the title essay in *A Small Personal Voice* (note 1), pp. 3-21, here p. 4; for the latter viewpoint see the interview by Christopher Bigsby in *The Radical Imagination and the Liberal Tradition. Interviews with English and American Novelists*, ed. Heide Ziegler and Christopher Bigsby (London: Junction, 1981), pp. 188-208, esp. p. 204f.

4. Letter from Doris Lessing to Mona Knapp, 12 June 1982.

5. Lessing, *Particularly Cats* (New York: Simon and Schuster, 1978), p. 86.

6. Cover blurbs from the paperback edition cited in note 2 above. All page references given in parentheses in the discussion of this work refer to this edition.

7. Title essay of *A Small Personal Voice* (note 1), p. 12.

8. Ibid., p. 17f.

9. In Lessing's 1967 Afterword (under the title "Eleven Years Later") to *Going Home* (New York: Popular Library, 1968), p. 252f.

10. Lessing's Foreword to Lawrence Vambe, *An Ill-Fated People: Zimbabwe Before and After Rhodes* (Pittsburgh: University of Pittsburgh Press, 1972), quoted here from the reprint in *Doris Lessing Newsletter* 4(1/1980), pp. 1, 11-13, here p. 12.

11. The anecdotes cited are found, respectively, in *A Small Personal Voice* (note 1), p. 158; the same volume, p. 137; and in the interview with Bigsby (note 3), p. 194.

12. From the cover text of *Going Home* (note 9). All page references in parentheses refer to this edition.

13. Interview with Lessing by Jonah Raskin in *A Small Personal Voice* (note 1), pp. 61-76, here p. 75.

14. As claimed by Jenny Taylor, "Introduction: Situating Reading," in *Notebooks/Memoirs/Archives. Reading and Rereading Doris Lessing*, ed. Jenny Taylor (Boston: Routledge & Kegan Paul, 1982), pp. 1-42, here p. 18.

15. Foreword to Vambe, *An Ill-Fated People* (note 10), here p. 11.

9. To Break Out of the Ordinary: Conclusion

1. Interview with Lessing by Lesley Hazleton, "Doris Lessing on Feminism, Communism and 'Space Fiction,' " *New York Times Magazine* 131(25 July 1982), p. 20ff.

2. Dee Seligman, *Doris Lessing. An Annotated Bibliography of Criticism* (Westport, Conn.: Greenwood Press, 1981).

3. D.B., *Doris Lessing* (New York: Twayne, 1965).

4. Cf. ibid., p. 39: "Justly—she knew that," or p. 103: "The tears that fill her eyes are of passionate regret." These lines, like the comparison to Dali (p. 17) and other observations, are Lessing's—only the quotation marks are missing.

5. P.S., *The Novels of Doris Lessing* (Carbondale: Southern Illinois University Press, 1973).

6. Schlueter makes it sound as if Mary's weak attempts to rebel against her husband and her situation could be censured as "unwise behavior" (p. 15); he sees Martha Quest (who lives to be nearly eighty) as entering her "last years" (p. 27) when she is thirty; when Martha is in labor she is described as "ill" (p. 62), etc.

7. Ellen Cronan Rose, *The Tree Outside the Window: Doris Lessing's* Children of Violence (Hanover, N.H.: University Press of New England, 1976).

8. Mary Ann Singleton, *The City and the Veld: The Fiction*

of *Doris Lessing* (Lewisburg: Bucknell University Press, 1977).

9. Michael Thorpe, *Doris Lessing's Africa* (London: Evans Brothers, 1978).

10. R.R., *The Novelistic Vision of Doris Lessing. Breaking the Forms of Consciousness* (Urbana: University of Illinois Press, 1979).

11. Paul Schlueter, ed., *The Fiction of Doris Lessing* (Evansville: University of Evansville Press, 1971).

12. A.P. and L.S.D., eds., *Doris Lessing. Critical Studies* (Madison: University of Wisconsin, 1974). Originally special issue of *Contemporary Literature* 14 (Fall 1973).

13. J.T., ed., *Notebooks/Memoirs/Archives. Reading and Rereading Doris Lessing* (Boston: Routledge & Kegan Paul, 1982).

14. The objectives of criticism are obscured, in my opinion, by musings on the nature of one's own love affairs while reading the text in question (p. 52); by opening an article with the assertion "I say I. I am going to say I. I claim the right to say I" (p. 75); or by ascertaining that Lessing is a "great lady" in an age when so much rubbish is being published (p. 123). These are but a few examples of overly personal methods.

15. Lessing, Afterword to *The Making of the Representative for Planet 8* (New York: Alfred A. Knopf, 1982), p. 134.

Bibliography

I. Major Works by Doris Lessing
(in chronological order)

The Grass is Singing. London: Michael Joseph, 1950.
This Was the Old Chief's Country. London: Michael Joseph, 1951.
Martha Quest (Children of Violence, Vol. 1). London: Michael Joseph, 1952.
Five: Short Novels. London: Michael Joseph, 1953.
A Proper Marriage (Children of Violence, Vol. 2). London: Michael Joseph, 1954.
Retreat to Innocence. London: Michael Joseph, 1956.
Going Home. London: Michael Joseph, 1957.
The Habit of Loving. London: MacGibbon and Kee, 1957.
A Ripple From the Storm (Children of Violence, Vol. 3). London: Michael Joseph, 1958.
Each His Own Wilderness. In *New English Dramatists. Three Plays*, ed. E. Martin Browne. Harmondsworth: Penguin, 1959.
Fourteen Poems. Northwood: Scorpion Press, 1959.
In Pursuit of the English. London: MacGibbon and Kee, 1960.
The Golden Notebook. London: Michael Joseph, 1962.
Play With a Tiger. London: Michael Joseph, 1962.
A Man and Two Women. London: MacGibbon and Kee, 1963.
African Stories. London: Michael Joseph, 1964.
Landlocked (Children of Violence, Vol. 4). London: Mac-Gibbon and Kee, 1965.
Particularly Cats. London: Michael Joseph, 1967.
The Four-Gated City (Children of Violence, Vol. 5). London: MacGibbon and Kee, 1969.
Briefing For a Descent Into Hell. London: Jonathan Cape, 1971.

The Story of a Non-Marrying Man and Other Stories. London: Jonathan Cape, 1972.

The Summer Before the Dark. London: Jonathan Cape, 1973.

This Was the Old Chief's Country (Collected African Stories, Vol. 1). London: Michael Joseph, 1973.

The Sun Between Their Feet (Collected African Stories, Vol. 2). London: Michael Joseph, 1973.

The Memoirs of a Survivor. London: Octagon Press, 1974.

A Small Personal Voice. Essays, Reviews, Interviews. Ed. Paul Schlueter. New York: Alfred A. Knopf, 1974.

To Room Nineteen (Collected Stories, Vol. 1). London: Jonathan Cape, 1978.

The Temptation of Jack Orkney (Collected Stories, Vol. 2). London: Jonathan Cape, 1978.

Stories. New York: Alfred A. Knopf, 1978.

Shikasta. Re: Colonised Planet 5 (Canopus in Argos: Archives, Vol. 1). New York: Alfred A. Knopf, 1979.

The Marriages Between Zones Three, Four, and Five. As Narrated by the Chroniclers of Zone Three (Canopus in Argos: Archives, Vol. 2). New York: Alfred A. Knopf, 1980.

The Sirian Experiments. The Report by Ambien II, of the Five (Canopus in Argos: Archives, Vol. 3). New York: Alfred A. Knopf, 1981.

The Making of the Representative for Planet 8 (Canopus in Argos: Archives, Vol. 4). New York: Alfred A. Knopf, 1982.

Documents Relating to the Sentimental Agents in the Volyen Empire (Canopus in Argos: Archives, Vol. 5). New York: Alfred A. Knopf, 1983.

II. Selected Critical Works on Lessing

Bibliographies

Burkom, Selma R., and Margaret Williams. *Doris Lessing: A Checklist of Primary and Secondary Sources.* Troy, N.Y.: Whitson Publishing Company, 1973.

Seligman, Dee. *Doris Lessing. An Annotated Bibliography of Criticism.* Westport, Conn.: Greenwood Press, 1981.

Monographs and Anthologies

Brewster, Dorothy. *Doris Lessing*. Twayne's English Authors
    Series, vol. 21. New York: Twayne, 1965.
Draine, Betsy. *Substance Under Pressure: Artistic Coherence
    and Evolving Forms in the Novels of Doris Lessing*. Madi-
    son: University of Wisconsin Press, 1983.
Holmquist, Ingrid. *From Society to Nature. A Study of Doris
    Lessing's* Children of Violence. Gothenburg Studies in En-
    glish, vol. 47. Göteborg, Sweden: Acta Universitatis
    Gothoburgensis, 1980.
Pratt, Annis, and L. S. Dembo, eds.: *Doris Lessing. Critical
    Studies*. Madison: University of Wisconsin Press, 1974.
    [Contains nine scholarly articles and an interview with
    Lessing; first published as a special issue of *Contemporary
    Literature* in Fall 1973.]
Rose, Ellen Cronan. *The Tree Outside the Window: Doris
    Lessing's* Children of Violence. Hanover, N.H.: University
    Press of New England, 1976.
Rubenstein, Roberta. *The Novelistic Vision of Doris Lessing.
    Breaking the Forms of Consciousness*. Urbana: University
    of Illinois Press, 1979.
Sage, Lorna. *Doris Lessing*. Contemporary Writers Series.
    New York: Methuen, 1983.
Schlueter, Paul, ed. *The Fiction of Doris Lessing*. Evansville:
    University of Evansville Press, 1971.
——. *The Novels of Doris Lessing*. Carbondale: Southern
    Illinois University Press, 1973.
Singleton, Mary Ann. *The City and the Veld. The Fiction of
    Doris Lessing*. Lewisburg: Bucknell University Press, 1977.
Taylor, Jenny, ed. *Notebooks/Memoirs/Archives. Reading
    and Rereading Doris Lessing*. Boston: Routledge & Kegan
    Paul, 1982. [Contains eight articles and an interview with
    the director of the film version of *Memoirs of a Survivor*.]

Selected Articles and Essays

For reasons of space, the many contributions in anthologies
(see above Pratt/Dembo, Schlueter 1971 and Taylor) and in
the *Doris Lessing Newsletter* will not be listed separately

here. The latter has published to date Volumes 1 (1976-77), 2 (1978), 3 (1979), 4 (1980), 5 (1981), 6 (1982), and 7 (1983). The reader is referred to this journal as a general source for essays, interviews and bibliographical information.

Brooks, Ellen W. "The Image of Woman in Lessing's *The Golden Notebook.*" *Critique* 15(1973): 101-109.

Brown, Lloyd W. "The Shape of Things: Sexual Images and the Sense of Form in Doris Lessing's Fiction." *World Literature Written in English* 14(1975): 176-186.

Burkom, Selma R. "Only Connect: Form and Content in the Works of Doris Lessing." *Critique* 11(1968): 51-68.

Chaffee, Patricia. "Spatial Patterns and Closed Groups in Lessing's *African Stories.*" *South Atlantic Bulletin* 43(1978): 42-52.

Drabble, Margaret. "Doris Lessing: Cassandra in a World Under Siege." *Ramparts* 10(1972): 50-54.

Draine, Betsy. "Changing Frames: Doris Lessing's *Memoirs of a Survivor.*" *Studies in the Novel* 11(1979): 51-62.

Gerver, Elisabeth. "Women Revolutionaries in the Novels of Nadine Gordimer and Doris Lessing." *World Literature Written in English* 17(1978): 38-50.

Gohlman, Susan A. "Martha Hesse of *The Four-Gated City:* A *Bildungsroman* Already Behind Her." *South Atlantic Bulletin* 43(1978): 95-107.

Hardin, Nancy Shields. "The Sufi Teaching Story and Doris Lessing." *Twentieth Century Literature* 23(1977): 314-325.

Howe, Florence. "Doris Lessing's Free Women." *The Nation*, 11 January 1965, pp. 34-37.

Joyner, Nancy. "The Underside of the Butterfly: Lessing's Debt to Woolf." *Journal of Narrative Technique* 4(1974): 204-212.

Kaplan, Sydney Janet. *Feminist Consciousness in the Modern British Novel.* Urbana: University of Illinois Press, 1975; on Lessing, pp. 136-172.

Karl, Frederick R. "Doris Lessing in the Sixties: The New Anatomy of Melancholy." *Contemporary Literature* 13 (1972): 15-33.

Krouse, Agate Nesaule. "Doris Lessing's Feminist Plays." *World Literature Written in English* 15(1976): 305-322.

Lardner, Susan. "An Angle on the Ordinary." *The New Yorker*, 19 September 1983, 140-154.

Lefcowitz, Barbara. "Dreams and Action in Lessing's *The Summer Before the Dark*." *Critique* 17(1975): 107-120.

Lightfoot, Marjorie J. " 'Fiction' vs. 'Reality': Clues and Conclusions in *The Golden Notebook*." *Modern British Literature* 2(1977): 182-188.

Magie, Michael L. "Doris Lessing and Romanticism." *College English* 38(1977): 531-552.

Marchino, Lois. "The Search for Self in the Novels of Doris Lessing." *Studies in the Novel* 4(1972): 252-261.

Markow, Alice Bradley. "The Pathology of Feminine Failure in the Fiction of Doris Lessing." *Critique* 16(1974): 88-100.

Mulkeen, Anne M. "Twentieth-Century Realism: The 'Grid' Structure of *The Golden Notebook*." *Studies in the Novel* 4 (1972): 262-274.

Porter, Dennis. "Realism and Failure in *The Golden Notebook*." *Modern Language Quarterly* 35(1974): 56-65.

Porter, Nancy. "Silenced History—*Children of Violence* and *The Golden Notebook*." *World Literature Written in English* 12(1973): 161-179.

———. "A Way of Looking at Doris Lessing." In *Female Studies VI*, ed. Nancy Hoffman, C. Secor, and A. Tinsley. New York: Feminist Press, 1972; pp. 123-138.

Pratt, Annis. "The Contrary Structure of Doris Lessing's *The Golden Notebook*." *World Literature Written in English* 12 (1973): 150-160.

Rapping, Elayne Antler. "Unfree Women: Feminism in Doris Lessing's Novels." *Women's Studies* 3(1975): 29-44.

Rose, Ellen Cronan. "The End of the Game: New Directions in Doris Lessing's Fiction." *Journal of Narrative Technique* 6(1976): 66-75.

Rubenstein, Roberta. "Briefing on Inner Space: Doris Lessing and R. D. Laing." *Psychoanalytic Review* 63(1976): 83-93.

———. "Doris Lessing's *The Golden Notebook*: The Meaning of its Shape." *American Imago* 32(1975): 40-58.

———. "Outer Space, Inner Space: Doris Lessing's Metaphor of Science Fiction." *World Literature Written in English* 14 (1975): 187-197.

Ryf, Robert S. "Beyond Ideology: Doris Lessing's Mature

Vision." *Modern Fiction Studies* 21(1975): 193-201.

Sarvan, Charles, and Sarvan, Liebetraut. "D.H. Lawrence and Doris Lessing's *The Grass is Singing.*" *Modern Fiction Studies* 24 (1978-79): 533-537.

Seligman, Dee. "The Sufi Quest." *World Literature Written in English* 12(1973): 190-206.

Showalter, Elaine. *A Literature of Their Own.* Princeton: Princeton University Press, 1977; on Lessing, pp. 298-319.

Spencer, Sharon. "Femininity and the Woman Writer: Doris Lessing's *The Golden Notebook* and the *Diary* of Anaïs Nin." *Women's Studies* 1(1973): 347-359.

Stitzel, Judith. "Reading Doris Lessing." *College English* 40 (1979): 498-504.

Vlastos, Marion. "Doris Lessing and R. D. Laing: Psychopolitics and Prophecy." *PMLA* 91(1976): 245-258.

Selected Interviews with Lessing

Bannon, Barbara A. "Authors and Editors." *Publishers Weekly* 195(2 June 1969), pp. 51-54.

Bigsby, Christopher. "Doris Lessing." In Heide Ziegler and Christopher Bigsby, eds., *The Radical Imagination and the Liberal Tradition. Interviews with English and American Novelists.* London: Junction, 1981; pp. 188-208.

Bikman, Minda. "A Talk With Doris Lessing." *New York Times Book Review*, 30 March 1980, pp. 1, 24-27.

Driver, C. J. "Profile 8: Doris Lessing." *The New Review* 1 (November 1974): 17-23.

Haas, Joseph. "Doris Lessing: Chronicler of the Cataclysm." *Chicago Sun Times* (*Panorama* Magazine) 14 June 1969, p. 4f.

Hazleton, Lesley. "Doris Lessing on Feminism, Communism and 'Space Fiction.' " *New York Times Magazine* 131 (25 July 1982), p. 20ff.

Oates, Joyce Carol. "A Visit With Doris Lessing." *The Southern Review* 9(1973): 873-882.

Wiseman, Thomas. "Mrs. Lessing's Kind of Life." *Time and Tide* 43(12 April 1962), p. 26.

Index

© ACC, 1977

Austin Community College
LEARNING RESOURCES CENTER
RIO GRANDE CAMPUS